# Old New England
# *Splint Baskets*
## *and how to make them*

John E. McGuire

*Schiffer Publishing Ltd*

77 Lower Valley Road, Atglen, PA 19310

## DEDICATION

To my parents and Sara
for their belief, love and support

## ACKNOWLEDGEMENTS

I am most thankful for the encouragement of friends and family who gave me the strength to sift through mountains of details and years of my life.

I am grateful to Michael J. Bartlett for allowing me to "swamp walk." My appreciation and gratitude to my business partner in Baskets and Bears, Chester D. Freeman, whose tireless efforts made this book a reality. My thanks to Joan Huntington for her warm hospitality and generosity in sharing her collection. Finally to Henry E. Peach whose gifted photography and welcomed advice helped make this book a visual delight.

All of the drawings and technical illustrations in this book were done by the author.

All photographs, including the front and back covers, were taken by Henry E. Peach.

Printed in China
ISBN: 0-88740-045-0

Published by Schiffer Publishing, Ltd.
77 Lower Valley Road
Atglen, PA 19310
Please write for a free catalog.
This book may be purchased from the publisher.
Please include $2.95 postage.
Try your bookstore first.

We are interested in hearing from authors
with book ideas on related subjects.

# Contents

*Preface* .................................................................................4
*A Historical Perspective* ...............................................5
*Tools*
    Antique Tools and Technology of Basketmaking .................9
    Modern Tools and Supplies need to make a new Basket ...........9
*Preparation*
    Identification and Ecology of the Black Ash tree ................14
        *Selecting a Tree* ..........................................15
        *Felling a Tree* ...........................................16
    Preparation of the Black Ash Log ..............................17
        *Pounding of the log* .....................................17
    Preparation of the Black Ash Splints .........................19
        *Cleaning* ................................................20
        *Dividing* ................................................20
        *Correcting uneveness* ....................................22
        *Sizing the weavers* ......................................22
        *Selecting material weight* ...............................23
    Preparation of Rim and Handle Stock ..........................23
        *Splitting out hickory for rims and handles* ..............23
        *Using white ash* .........................................26
    Carving Rims and Handles from Hickory .......................26
        *Carving the rim* .........................................26
        *Carving the handle* ......................................27
*Making a Basket*
    Round Basket .................................................31
    Rectangular Basket ...........................................46
    Square to Round Basket .......................................51
    Inserting the Handle .........................................53
    Fitting the Rims .............................................53
    Lashing the Basket ...........................................57
    Lacing .......................................................63
*Antique Baskets* .......................................................66
*Glossary* ..............................................................92
*Useful Information*
    Newsletters and other Publications related to Basketry ......94
    Newspapers for the Basketmaker and Basket Collector .........94
    Branding Supplies ...........................................95
    Marketing for the Professional Basketmaker ..................95
    Resources for your Personal Library .........................95

# Preface

This is the first comprehensive book on traditional New England black ash splint baskets and the basketmaking process. The purposes of this book are:

- to provide insights into the historical disputes regarding basketmaking and its technology
- to teach the basic skills needed to make traditional New England basket forms using historical material and techniques
- to enable an individual to analyze a basket, be it modern or antique, thereby creating a more informed and appreciative buyer
- to encourage individual style and creativity in basketmaking based on the fundamental weaving process
- to present useful information and resources for basketmakers and collectors
- to serve as a reference insuring that this tradition of basketmaking will be passed on to other generations

For the basket fancier this book offers a privileged look at some outstanding examples of antique baskets and tools. These photographs and drawings are included to provide both inspiration and a visual treat. I have specifically eliminated measurements to allow the viewer and maker an opportunity to interpret form without being bound to size. Laborious recreations can both hamper creativity and spontaniety.

For the novice or skilled basketmaker who has never before used black ash splint, I invite you to experience the enchantment of making a basket from a tree.

While black ash is unavailable in certain geographic regions, the quest for this elusive material either through personal explorations and travel or buying it through individuals and suppliers will prove worthwhile. The delicate sophistication attainable coupled with the integral strength achieved makes this material ideal and magical.

Should you choose to use alternate material such as commercial flat reed, white ash, oak, hickory or harvested cat tail leaves, the basics of the weaving process remain constant. This book is loaded with tips, hints and useful information which I have gleaned through my experience of teaching. The techniques that so distinguish antique baskets of New England as collectible art forms are combined with imaginative contemporary adaptations for modern basket enthusiasts. All of this knowledge along with the often jealously guarded secrets of basketmaking establish this book as a classic reference.

*Basket Peddler*
*Woodcut circa 1825*
*Alexander Anderson*
*Print Collection*
*The New York Public Library*
*Astor, Lenox and Tilden Foundations*

# A Historical Perspective

Perhaps the single largest benefit working as a teaching interpreter of basketmaking history is that, along with the clothes, one "becomes" the basketmaker of the 1830s. Now I walk in his shoes and can begin to relive what a man's role as basketmaker was about. Historically most were men in New England white society with Shaker and Native American women being a distinct exception.

I relive his drudgery of selecting black ash logs, removing them from swampy lands, taking off the bark and hand pounding loose the growth rings from successive layers of the tree. I can understand the wish for sons or helpers who could minimize this most unpleasant task.

When I enter the blacksmith shop in our village I experience the envy that must have happened if he encountered an triphammer. Along with the pain came the pleasure of a trade—the demand for baskets and their repair was beginning to reach full time proportions. Unlike the earliest days of our country, survival is not the issue and so a basketmaker could now conceivably sustain himself in this trade with some obvious farming; and in fact even have helpers and become a "manufacturer" selling to the public either directly, through peddlers who buy and resell or through stores doing the same.

Annually he could make $250 a year—certainly above the average fifty cents per day wage that a laborer would make on a farm. Prices of baskets seem to receive a great deal of attention and speculation. Certainly this $250 income was far from outstanding but it was enough for survival. The marketplace surely set limits on how much a person would pay for a basket. No one could ever have a monopoly on product or price. New England was far too progressive and competitive to allow this to happen. Yet journals show a wide range of prices from a few cents to over one dollar. Obviously price varied according to sizes but quality must have been the determining factor.

Finely woven, substantial heft of materials to insure longevity, skids or runners on the bottom to protect, and securely lashed rims all spoke of the skill of the maker and the worth of owning. I feel the bulk of baskets were sold in the fifteen cents to fourty cents range. Naturally a maker had physical limits on the numbers of baskets he could produce annually. Once I encountered a report of a maker who "crowed" at the fact he could average three baskets a day. Naturally this didn't mean he started and finished the same three on a single day. Drying and tightening of materials were necessary, hence the need for many baskets at many stages of completion.

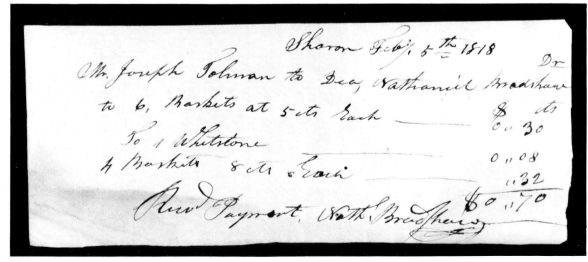

Basket receipt
Author's Collection

Not including repairs, which would somewhat lower the average price, simple mathematics show 3 per day x 6 days per week x 52 weeks divided into $250 annually equals 26 cents. This is a rather substantial price, so these baskets weren't small baskets at a big price—New Englanders were too practical to be fleeced. If a prospective buyer didn't like the price I am sure the marketplace allowed him or her a choice. Perhaps he or she might wait to buy a Shaker or Native American basket that would be brought to the area by the Shaker representatives or Indians. These baskets were finely crafted, often mould woven and because they lived in community, their survival was somewhat insured. Hence they might be below market price. When this happened a local maker lost sales but numbers of needed baskets couldn't be met by these competitors. Thus the laws of supply and demand again took over.

An introduction to basketmaking could have happened either generationally, through helping another maker, marriage to an Algonkian Indian or simply a person's own skills. Regardless of the way a basketmaker was trained I believe that like many makers production was paramount.

This trade lent itself to part-timers who could make baskets in winter or itinerants and so this interaction also kept prices, sizes and quality in line; not to mention standarized weights and measures now used to test baskets should someone think a maker was not producing an honest bushel. All of the demands for sizes led to the use of moulds—insuring uniformity but also raising output. No longer need a maker struggle to turn corners neatly or free-form a certain shape. They simply pulled the material tight to the mould and the work was done. It is this technology and the origin of the use of black ash that divides scholars and curators.

As a basketmaker first and historian second, my theory is one of practical knowledge. Moulds simply make sense—something that abounds in practical people. I have never doubted that "splits" (splints) were part of our European basket tradition. My contention is that with little time for innovation in techniques and with the unpleasantness of searching swamps for black ash—the white settlers did not "discover" black ash. Rather, the Native Americans told the white settlers about it. Certainly there were enough hardwoods being cleared from future farmlands that hunting for basketwood was a waste of the white settler's valued time. The pounding of oak, hickory or other basketwoods would have proved fruitless, but the pounding of black ash yields uniform strips the length of the tree with a minimum of wasted materials not to mention the unnecessary "dressing" of the splints to a particular thickness. Black ash can be readily divided and subdivided to almost paper thinness without the waste of materials or time. I believe the Native New England Indians, whose baskets "handsomely and cunningly made,"[1] had already learned the secrets of black ash.

One could use the work of Speck (1947)[2] to support this theory if the terms "woodsplints" and "ash splints" can be equated in Native American basketry.

The earliest American recorded writing mentioning woodsplint basketry is dated 1712[3] and it mentions teaching the Native Americans of the Delaware Valley basketry. However, I believe that these were only stylistic innovations—something the Native Americans gave back in equal measure with one unparalled plus—the use of black ash and its preparation. Scholars may never settle this issue especially when the oral tradition of the Native Americans leave us without "hard" evidence, but one only needs to study the ecology of black ash and experience its uniqueness to making baskets to settle this issue at least personally.

The same controversy swirls around the use of basket moulds—their numbers depleted by use or burning by an unaware public. Yet enough survive to show their impact on basketmaking.

Shaker baskets began to appear for resale in the early 1800s with their wide acceptance by 1837. Mount Lebanon account books show seventy-six styles being produced—most on moulds. Artifact Shaker baskets can be clearly matched to numerous antique moulds that are preserved in Shaker museums. This technology appears to have evolved through interactions of the Shaker community with the Native New England community on a give and take basis. While the Shakers were unique, this technology was hardly theirs alone. When Abner Baily died in Mansfield, Massachusetts in 1837, his machinery and moulds evidenc

6

his proliferated technology.[4] Again hard evidence, while existant, is sparce and scholars want more rather than less to prove theories. I too wish for more than isolated evidence but as a basketmaker I let my practical side as a weaver and maker of functional items be the judge. One basket free-hand is worth three on a mould in effort, but from an aesthetic, business or buyer approach I will choose a moulded basket. Some New England historical societies have examples of these tools and technology. During my research at the Connecticut Historical Society I found the account book and tools of Joseph Codding.[5] Though his account book is dated 1869, his tools and moulds are not unlike those of Abner Bailey. It seems inexplicable that this technology would be developed during a period when mechanization and basket factories are emerging. The individual maker was already experiencing disruptive change in the market-place. I believe these tools must have been in place giving him the hope that he might "hang on."

My final question is why would a basketmaker develop the use of basket moulds and machinery in a trade that made few makers rich and that by the end of 1800 suffered a shift from widespread manufacturing to a craft? I rather think it makes more sense that the moulds, slitters and other tools so documented in the later part of the 1800s were part of a generational inheritance that evidenced itself in basketmaking lineage until the basket-makers simply fell victim to modern technology. I continue to struggle with these theories. Both sides are still at odds about much of basketmaking technology but we each continue to shed light on the subject.

**NOTES**

William Bradford. *Homes in the Wilderness: A Pilgrim's Journal of the Plimoth Plantation in 1620.* New York: William R. Scott, Inc., 1939.

Frank G. Speck. *Eastern Algonkian Block-Stamp Decoration.* New Jersey: The Archeological Society of New Jersey, 1947.

Regarding the origin of the use of black ash splint in basketmaking, there are two schools of thought. Some scholars theorize that the Native New England Indians used woodsplints and were pounding logs long before the European settlers arrived. The author uses this theory held by Frank G. Speck to support his thesis. The other contention is held by Ted. J. Brasser and he theorizes that the Native Americans were taught black ash splint basketry by the Swedish and German settlers in the Delaware Valley during the 17th and 18th centuries and that they adapted this technique of making baskets instead of their twined basketry tradition. If you are interested in pursuing these theories please consult the above reference to Speck and T.J. Brasser. *A Basketful of Indian Culture Change.* Ottowa: Canada Ethnology Service: 22, 1975.

[4]*Middleborough Antiquarian.* "Basketmaking in New England in the 19th Century," April 1966.

[5]Account book, tools (including shavehorse) and baskets of Joseph Codding are found in the collection of the Connecticut Historical Society. Mr. Codding was a native of Danielson, Connecticut and lived from 1834-1909.

# Tools

## ANTIQUE TOOLS AND TECHNOLOGY OF BASKETMAKING

Once you begin to seriously look at baskets you, will be amazed at the amount of information you can glean. Suddenly this wooden form begins to tell us something about its age, maker, and production techniques.

The first real problem is accurately determining age. Obviously if a basket is dated and carries with it appropriate darkening (patina) and wear, anyone can say definitely that it was made at that time. However as prices climb and "faking" begins to be worthwhile the genius of the forgery will become difficult to detect.

Historically, painting of baskets by users was exclusively the only finish applied except with the Nantucket Lightship baskets which were shellacked.[6] These aged painted baskets now command the highest prices in the antique world and help us confirm a basket's age. Until recently the use of a "black light" or ultraviolet light has revealed newly aged paint through its fluorescent appearance. Modern technology and creativity has eliminated this bit of detection so now the buyer or collector needs more than science; he needs knowledge of materials, construction techniques and a logical mind always on guard.

Linings in a basket can also give clues. Fabrics of the period or newspapers added to protect a basket can give valuable insight. Here again old materials can be added to the new fakes so someone needs to look at how this lining is secured. Sewing or pasting it in place was the only way within reason until modern times. Old glues have a different look and smell and thread ages along with everything else—so look for evidence that it was there—not added. Protected splint carries a fresh color so move a splint and look for newness. Thread also shields a fabric at the point of over-

*Keep accurate records on the baskets in your collection.*

cast. Uniform color or space-age technology spells new. That isn't to say new isn't good and worth serious investment, just be aware of what you are buying.

Now that you are over that hurdle, look again at the basket and more will unfold. If a basket narrows at the top more than the body and it is perfectly symmetrical—one might assume a puzzle mould was used. I do not wish to infer that makers are incapable of such perfection, but moulds make it faster and add a beauty of uniformity not mandated except in "measures" but appreciated by the buyer. A beautiful, well-constructed competitively priced basket would surely be everyone's first choice. Ugly was not ever popular—unless you made it yourself for yourself.

Perfectly cut splint suggested a slitting tool that sized materials for weaving. Cutting everything by hand and eye could quickly lead you to a new occupation. A large, perfectly shaped basket woven with delicately thin materials speaks artistic touch or a practical person dividing his or her materials, or both. The beauty of ash, especially black (brown) ash, is that this material can be subdivided exposing its satiny interior.

Strongly grained splint in uniformly thin splint is further evidence of the use of machinery. Around 1850 a basketmaker developed a veneering machine that eliminated a good deal of hand work. Anticipating helping his fellow basketmakers, he gave a boost to baskets and emerging factories and unexpectedly hurt the individual maker. The demand for baskets grew but factories kept a price lid on everyone's products—now supply and demand ruled the market. As other containers evolved the need for baskets slacked—prices stabilized or fell

*Nailed and stapled rims are a sign of newer baskets.*
*Finishes or waxes should not be applied to old baskets as it can destroy their value. Simple cleaning and proper care will increase a basket's longevity. When in doubt, consult an expert.*

and a once-important industry turned into a now-important craft. This veneered splint still is available but its limitations in strength and sophistication make "making your own" or buying reed a viable alternative.

The following section reveals pen and ink drawings of many of the tools found in museums, historical societies and private collections. Aside from curiosities, they also have contemporary applications. In most instances I will attempt to point out their relevance; however, this section invites your creativity to adapt and adopt.

## THE UNIVERSAL TOOL—A BASKET-MAKER'S HANDS

The most basic tools are one's hands. Without strong hands the basketmaker was never going to succeed. Lore has it that with his hands and a knife a basketmaker was in business. While true, I wouldn't wish to prove this statement on a regular basis. As man's ingenuity extended to auxilary tools his labor, while strenuous, began to become efficiently applied. All of the following tools are not necessary but a production maker may well have possessed them all and *more*.

### THE BARK SPUD

While not an essential, this blacksmith-produced tool helped the basketmaker remove bark from his logs. Slighly curved to hug the curve of the log, it facilitates this process. Today they have been found offered in flea markets often mistakenly identified as tools for whaling, but almost always at a reasonable price ($18-30).

### THE FROE

An invaluable tool, again produced by the blacksmith, the froe is available at flea markets or contemporary wood-supply catalogs for $25-40. The cutting edge is placed against the wood and the top surface of the blade is struck with a mallet (froe club). The force of the club drives the blade into the wood. Then the handle is moved from side to side until the piece is split in half. This process is repeated until long pieces approximately 1" square are obtained.

Trees split for handles are usually begun with a wedge and sledge. The smaller pieces are then split in halves with the froe (after removing the heart-wood—darker center wood) until the desired size is achieved. It is helpful if, in splitting, you start at the narrow (top) end of the wood and *always remember to divide in half either across or with the grain of the wood. If the split starts off poorly, quit and attempt the other end.*

### FROE CLUB

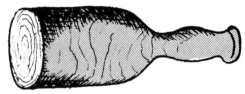

This doubles as a mallet to pound splint. Available in many woods and conditions, they vary in price from $8-35. A black (brown) ash is felled, debarked and then methodically, rhythmically, and completely beaten to separate the growth rings one at a time. Each ring in then peeled from the log in a lengthwise fashion. If every square inch of the log is prepared so as to freely allow splint to be removed *without* pulling—each successive layer will require progressively less work. A log will yield hundreds of splints for basketmaking. This material is sometimes offered for sale but is not to be confused with veneered ash splint which is prepared differently and "works" differently.

### SPLINT SLITTERS (GAUGES)

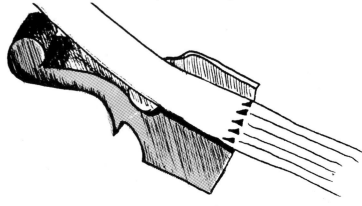

These hand-carved tools are seldom found in antique shows and always carry a fairly high price depending on condition... ($40-125). They were used to prepare weaving materials of uniform size. These slitters came in series with the cutting blades (sharpened clock spring) set at desired cutting intervals. This razor-sharp, extremely thin metal facilitates cutting and minimized drag on the splint—allowing the material to be pulled through easily.

The drawing shows a fanciful gauge requiring a thumb's pressure to keep the splint "down" and engaged in the blades. The blades are held in place by a metal plate across the front eliminating their being pulled forward and out of the handle. Others had swivel or permanent bars that hold the splint down with the high sides preventing lateral movement. These thin blades also allowed material to be cut in straight lines and in some cases across a twisted grain thus maximizing splint.

Most often I use a reproduction of this tool but on the occasion I use the antique, I have found clock spring superior to razor blades. Antique Native American gauges tend to be among the most beautiful and prized but all are relatively scarce and collectible. Modern leather catalogs offer an adjustable leather stripper that generally suits today's needs at around $24.00, with replaceable blades. This machine works well with moist straight grain splint.

## MOULDS (MOLDS)

Moulds (molds) are also known as drums or forms. These carry a higher than average price at antique shows ($30-100). Individually produced or made by a woodworker, these forms came in dozens of shapes. They were often discarded or burned by an unknowing public. Constructed of solid wood or slats with tops and bottoms, these forms were easily removed from the baskets. Most forms can be classified into three categories: 1) Solid, 2) Built-Up and 3) Puzzle. All are illustrated.

## BASKETMAKING MACHINES

While there is not a machine that weaves a basket, there are now and were "machines" that assisted the basketmaker in producing baskets. From very simple to extremely sophisticated forms, these "machines" were designed to accept moulds which were rotated by the maker to allow for easier weaving. A number of these machines reside in collections of several museums and while seldom on view are most ingenious. The variety ranged from simple posts with holes to receive the stem of a mould to fixed stems that fit holes in the bottom of the moulds allowing for rotation.

Unfortunately many exhibits incorrectly mix various types of basketry tools in an attempt to show construction techniques.

## KNIFE

The basketmaker's knife was made of heavy steel sometimes with a small curved end resembling a flat hook. Referred to as a crooked knife, it was used to help separate splints. Exquisite antique Native American examples are highly sought after by collectors ($65-150).

*Dry splint, when cut, may crack. Splint used in a moistened state minimizes this problem.*

## SCISSORS

Scissors were hand forged and again available in antique shows ($20-45). The importance of scissors can not be under-estimated.

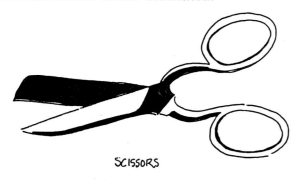

SCISSORS

## CLAMPS

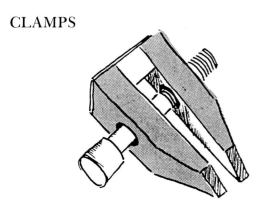

An endless variety of clamps were developed for multiple uses. No specific type or size of clamp was unique to the basketmaker; they obviously varied according to the job. Wood clamps were created by using tap and die sets and were logically employed to hold the rim ends together to facilitate final lashing of a basket. The price varies according to styles and condition ($10-30).

## SAW

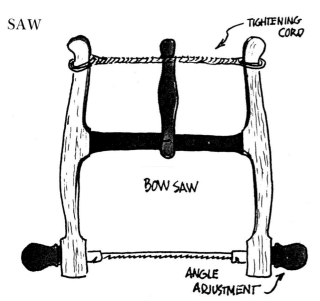

TIGHTENING CORD

BOW SAW

ANGLE ADJUSTMENT

Made in a variety of styles, the saw was used to notch handles and cut materials to length. The style illustrated is commonly known as a bow saw. These handsome tools are still found in the antique marketplace and range from $65-100.

## DRAWKNIFE AND SHAVEHORSE

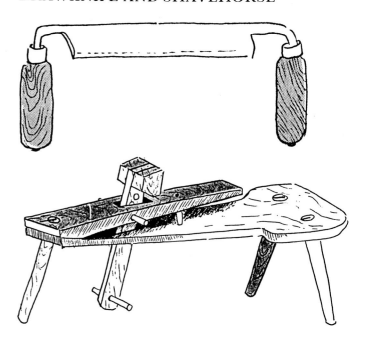

These two tools, when used in tandem, produced the carved and cleaned parts of baskets with greater speed. The shavehorse is nothing more than a clamp that operates through a foot pedal. By pushing the foot forward, the operator makes the head or block pivot forward to hold the material against a flat shaving plane. Still available in antique shows, ($100-225) they range in price depending on the condition.

The shavehorse was used in a variety of woodworking processes, so thought must be given to its utility. The shaving surface should be long enough to support the material and give a reference surface to the worker.

The drawknife is merely a two handled knife that straddles the width of the shaving surface. Again available in flea markets ($15-40) or available new in woodworking catalogs, these sturdy tools allow a basketmaker to quickly develop a touch in carving that liberates a maker from endless drudgery. Large drawknives are more common but hamper delicate carving except by the most experienced worker. Generally the smaller the knife the easier it is to control.

The values given in this book for basketmaking collectibles should be used only as a guideline. Naturally they will vary depending on the condition and demand of the object and the area in which you live.

## MODERN TOOLS AND SUPPLIES NEEDED TO MAKE A NEW BASKET

*The number of tools you choose to buy and use depends directly on your needs.*

### The real necessities are:

| | |
|---|---|
| a piece of leather or canvas large enough to cover your knee | sharp scissors |
| | tape measure |
| | two clamps |
| strong sharp jackknife | small saw |
| #2 lead pencil | |

### The options are:

| | |
|---|---|
| Knife (crooked) | tightening stick |
| branding iron | flat bladed knife |
| spray bottle | drawknife |
| wooden mallet | tweezers |
| froe | waterproof pen |
| slitting gauges | increment borer |
| dividing box | paint scraper |
| screwdriver | shavehorse |

While I mention and use nearly all the tools in both lists they are by NO MEANS A MUST. As you begin to expand your involvement in basketry you can add them as you go.

Expensive tools are not necessary. It is their care and use which make the difference. Individual creativity augments basket aesthetics and maximizes the enjoyment for the maker. Not every apartment-dweller has space for a shavehorse and as far as beauty, they do little to enhance a decor. A substitution can be found using your ingenuity. Perhaps "C" clamps and a collapsible sawhorse can be used. The wise use of a saw and a jackknife can make the most elaborate handle—where there is a will there is a way. Obtaining fresh wood can be a problem, yet a call to the local department of public works (DPW) or forestry service can put you on the trail of tree trimmings.

If you wish to soak these limbs, a tub is perfect or a piece of 4" PVC pipe with an end cap glued in place. This water-tight cylinder can store a quantity of wood vertically and the water can easily be changed or kept fresh with periodic additions of bleach. Should you choose to let your wood dry, an end-capped piece of household galvanized metal gutter can be placed across two burners so that a basket handle can be boiled for bending. I have on occasion carefully used my microwave to heat up a piece of fresh "wet" wood for bending. Obviously using a microwave on dry wood will produce nothing at best or a FIRE AT WORST! The human spirit and imagination can provide the direction and a good building supply store the resource. Make the best of your tools, learn how to maintain them and keep them sharp.

A number of companies are beginning to offer ever widening varieties of supplies. Basketry was at one time a craft that tested the new maker's creativity but now it requires selectivity. I have included a directory of suppliers for your convenience but in no way can I vouch for the quality of the product or the company. I strongly advise you to visit your local suppliers and *examine the materials before you buy them.* If ordering by mail choose companies which allow returns.

---

*Build a shavehorse. See "Fine Woodworking Magazine" September 1978.*
*Make your own drawknife. For instructions see the author's article in "The News Basket" June 1985.*

**NOTES**
[6]Not to be confused with Native American woodsplint baskets which were swabbed and decorated.

# Preparation

## IDENTIFICATION AND ECOLOGY OF THE BLACK ASH TREE (THE BASKET TREE)

The black ash tree takes its name from the dark brown heartwood and is the northern-most native ash. This ash tree has a variety of nicknames: basket ash, basket tree, hoop ash and brown ash to name a few. The *Fraxinus nigra* (black ash) is found in the wet soils of cold swamps and peat bogs where drainage is poor and also within the boundaries of coniferous and hardwood forests. These trees do not flourish in stagnant water. Some water movement (drainage) is necessary. When endangered or at the end of its growth cycle, ash proliferates through seeding. Should you locate remnants of black ash continue to check downstream and in the direction of the prevailing winds.

Because of its habitat it is rare to encounter a black ash tree that reaches over one foot in diameter. Due to its struggle for survival, it often appears to be "half sick" near the top. Its silhouette without leaves appears to fit the usual requirements for a "horror movie." The strong thick branches of the tree are found in a crown at the top with an absence of small twigs. The 7-11 leaflets are opposite each other and attach directly (no leaf stalk) to a central 12-16" lead stem. Individual leaves are broad and lance-shaped with finely serrated edges.

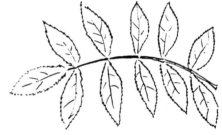

The tree bears fruit (seeds) which hang in clusters and mature in late summer.

Its bark is most distinctive and has been said to resemble that of elm. It is gray in color, corky in nature and fissured into soft scaly plates. These scales rub off easily, a characteristic peculiar to this tree.

The black ash has a normal growing range southeast of Manitoba and east to Newfoundland, as far south as West Virginia, and as far west as Iowa. Black ash grows in altitudes of up to 3500 feet above sea level.

One of the reasons so few people use black ash is their unfamiliarity with the tree and its unique material. Once found in large numbers, this species suffered a significant decline in the 1800's partially from its popular use in basketry. Coupled with ecological damage, decline through natural causes, and disuse due to alternate material choices, the black ash all but vanished in its use for baskets. A renaissance now seems in the making with the marketing of black ash splint—a difficult but potentially profitable business. There have been "purists" who have always used this special "New England ash" and to these people I feel modern basketmakers owe a debt of gratitude.

To those of you who have a sense of history and adventure, the black ash can still be found and enjoyed. The following will lead you through the process of locating a black ash tree and preparing your own splint. Additional information is given for those who wish to find alternate raw materials.

SELECTING A TREE

Because of its habitat and the probable excitement of pursuit, it is always smart to be a bit cautious. Spring is perhaps the best time to cut and identify black ash but winter is the best time to do your scouting. First familiarize yourself with the area you are going to enter. Topographical maps may help give you an overview and show you where to look. A forestry manager or woodsman can be your best help.

Next obtain permission to "swamp walk" and do not go alone! You will need help should you find a tree. Permission is your legal protection, and two heads are better than one for marking trails and emerging safely. A saw and boots should be part of your equipment and a will to succeed your driving force—not to mention the beautiful baskets waiting to be made. Walking for a tree is a time of both peaceful searching and exhilaration.

Once you find what you think is a black ash tree go through this checklist:

1. Bark        scaly-corky that flakes or rubs off
2. Color       gray but with great variety of color depending on growing conditions

*When looking for a black ash tree in the winter time the buds of the tree are blue-black. In the spring time the flowers of the tree appear purplish.*

| | |
|---|---|
| 3. Top Appearance | crown: half-sick appearance; no fine branches |
| 4. Leaf | usually high up; check it against the description if possible |

If you are reasonably sure you have the right kind of tree, you must select the best one for cutting. Enthusiasm of discovery doesn't mean the end of the hunt. Through damage by wildlife or other natural cause, this tree may not be the best one to cut. The big advantage is that black ash seldom grows alone; where there is one, there often are many.

Look for the straightest tree with a blemish-free, healthy trunk. Mature black ash seldom has low branches, yet evidence of low branches in the bark is to be avoided. A knot at the surface spells extra work and only great frustration as you pound splint. Look *carefully* for the right tree that affords you a log ideally 10-12 feet long which is knot-free. In many cases this may not be possible, so carefully select the best available; a wasted tree helps no one, especially the species. Use an increment borer to remove a plug to examine the health of the tree and its pattern of growth rings. This greatly facilitates your choice.

## FELLING A TREE

The tree should be cut about one foot off the ground and the trunk reserved. After the log is cut, the remainder of the tree should be removed and used, or can be cut up in sections with the limbs removed to allow the wood to return to the soil more quickly. Leave your area as clean and undamaged as possible. For those with wood stoves, the neglected parts of the log make good firewood.

As previously stated, the ideal time to cut the log is the spring when the sap is rising in the tree. A log usually "pounds out" regardless of the time of the year it is cut, but should it resist easy preparation you can always submerge it in water and weigh it down. The soaking process can be done for up to one year and greatly helps a stubborn log; any longer is questionable. Some trees tend to be brittle and if the splint remains unmanageable after the soaking process, the log is best used as an alternate choice for rims and handles, or burned. In any case the log just cut should not be allowed to dry—so either get the job over and completely pound out the splint or find a pond or stream to submerge the log. Should neither natural water source exist, a simple wood frame lined with heavy plastic and filled with water should suffice. Periodic addition of bleach helps retard bacterial growth and makes your job more pleasant.

The last issue is price. Many property owners feel that anyone who will go through such perseverance earns this log for their toil. For those of you who are asked to pay, I would like to acquaint you with a bit of New England tradition. The basket tree got its nickname because a basketmaker offered a basket of personal choice to the owner of the tree. It was a good bargain for all concerned, the owner got an item of utility and the maker got the remaining raw materials. Most tree owners are both intrigued with this story and delighted with owning a basket from a tree they would seldom, if

*A number of fatalities occur annually due to the inexperience of persons when felling a tree. Contact a professional forestry manager and learn as much about the process before attempting to do it. NEVER GO ALONE IN THE FOREST. YOU WILL ALWAYS NEED ASSISTANCE.*

ever, use. If this bit of history doesn't delight the seller, then a price of $10.00 to $40.00 should be sufficient.

## PREPARATION OF THE BLACK ASH LOG

### POUNDING THE LOG

Upon its arrival home the log should immediately be prepared and "pounded." The bark spud or drawknife is used to remove the bark.

Next the exposed log is struck with a wooden mallet or maul. Contemporary splint producers use pipe, the back of an axe or a sledge to do their pounding. Naturally, the heavier the blow, the faster the work; this concept works up to a point. Obviously, a light blow will minimize efficiency but too-hard a blow can waste your whole effort. Instead of crushing the fibers between the growth rings, an over-zealous person can fracture the splint reducing its utility. The more fractures the more difficult it is to obtain the clear grain that so facilitates weaving. The only case where more is better is in preparation time on the log. It is this author's opinion that a fairly heavy wooden mallet (Hornbeam) comfortable to the grip and lift is useful for this job.

Place the log on end supports at a comfortable level. You want your pounding to be absorbed by the log, not the ground. It is at this point that your sense of rhythm, patience, fortitude and desire take over. The log needs to be uniformly, methodically and lovingly struck.

Overlapping your blows will insure proper preparation. ONE WORD OF WARNING—LET THE WEIGHT OF THE MALLET DO THE WORK—LET THE WRIST RELAX PRIOR TO IMPACT. FORCING OR "DRIVING" THE MALLET CAN ONLY INJURE YOUR HANDS AND TENDONS!

The joy of that first perfect splint replaces the agony of blisters and sore muscles. Keep band-aids available until you toughen up your hands, and always remember: the extra effort you initially spend on the first few layers of splint show up in later effort. The shock waves that are sent into the log help loosen the entire log. I have estimated that the first layer takes approximately *16 blows per square inch* and because this is just below the bark, it may not produce useable material. Hopefully the next layer and beyond will produce the splint you are after. A good log will yield splint until the center of the log and small knots render it useless. Some makers, however, use the center material for rims and handles in place of hardwoods.

---

*Native Americans coated a log with mud to show where their pounding stopped as well as to prevent the log from drying out.*
*When pounding splint with a wooden mallet, your growth rings on the mallet should be perpendicular to the pounding surface and impact blows should overlap each other.*

I have found a considerable difference in the quality of logs. In areas where growing conditions are optimum such as in Canada or near the Canadian border in the United States, a good tree will respond as previously described. Recently I have been cutting trees in both Massachusetts and Connecticut and find that a considerable number of very poor growing years characterize these logs. It appears that the paper-thin growth rings of the last 10-15 years must be carefully removed with a drawknife before the pounding produces successful splint preparation. The log will also release splint that varies in thickness within a specific growth ring. This variation is produced by the tree's exposure to direct sun versus the shaded side of the tree. These variations all can be incorporated into the production of various elements of the basket.

The nearer to the tree's center, the darker the wood and some makers use various colors of wood splints to produce contrasts in their baskets. This natural beauty diminishes as the basket begins to darken and take on that rich brown patina. It is this rich brown color that reed basketmakers simulate through dyes. Regardless of your sense of design, this long lasting quality of black (brown) ash only looks better with age.

Lastly, the width of the strips should be what is easy to handle because this splint is to be cut down into usable sizes. Large sheets of wood are unnecessary. Occasional scoring with a knife may facilitate the peeling and sizing process.

White ash, which is more readily available, also can be prepared in the same fashion. These splints however, handle similiarly but produce a less supple basket and the pounding process is more labor-intensive. For more information see the chapter on the Preparation of Rim and Handle Stock.

## PREPARATION OF THE BLACK ASH SPLINTS

Once the splint is removed from the log it can be allowed to dry until needed. I find that it is easier to store splint if it is coiled up into bundles of 5-8 splints. It should be stored in a cool dry place and allowed to dry in order to prevent mildew from discoloring the splint. Normally a bundle of splint can make at least one basket and requires little time to soak before use. Unlike reed, which should soak 3-5 minutes and then be wrapped in a moist towel, this splint can remain soaking almost indefinitely. The only problem, if such, is that the wood "grays" just as does an unprotected shingle on a

*Commercially prepared oak and white ash is often available in supply stores. Watch sharp bends when using this for basketry.*
*Oak and similiar hardwoods are not pounded to produce splint.*

roof. The ash strips require further preparation and sizing to be used successfully in basketmaking.

Upon closer examination there are coarse outer fibers that cling to the splint. These fibers are what were crushed in the pounding process and represent the nourishing network of the tree laid down at the various growth intervals. Uncleaned splint can be worked by simply cutting it into desired strips suitable to the basket in production. If this coarseness is offensive or detracts from the aesthetics of the basket it can be removed. Using a flat bladed knife and a piece of leather on your thigh, the blade is held in a nearly flat angle to the splint and the material is pulled through the blade scraping the splint clean.

It is important to note that the knife is held *stationary* and the leather helps you slide the splint through the knife. This process requires mastery. Too vertical an angle and little is accomplished—too sharp or too fast a motion and the splint is cut in two pieces. Other cleaning alternatives are a paint scraper that has been sharpened or a thickness sander. While available in "kits," these sanders are not necessary and are expensive.

*Buy a flat bladed knife. This can be used for all your carving and cleaning needs.*
*Avoid frequent soaking and drying of reed (flat). It tends to create weakness and splitting.*

## CLEANING

When cleaning by hand, you will quickly notice that these fibrous materials clean off better on one side than the other; and they have a seemingly pronounced direction. Holding a knife and pulling the material through the knife edge, these fibers seem to resist removal—WHEN THE DIRECTION IS REVERSED THE FIBERS CAN BE REMOVED MORE EFFICIENTLY. As a person becomes skilled, the process is quickly done. It is accomplished in almost a continuous motion without damaging the surface thickness. The outside of the splint that would be closest to the bark is the side that cleans the easiest.

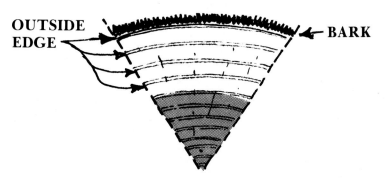

When you look at a strip of splint, the curved up-surface, when moistened, flattens easier and allows for cleaning from edge to edge. The opposite side resists somewhat and many beginners seem to have cleaned edges but little else. A balance will be developed with practice. I might add, a very supportive friend and now retired basketmaker, Mary Tilley, seldom cleaned weavers or uprights. Crowned with beautiful handles and rims, her baskets were classics. Baskets, fortunately, and black ash especially, allow for individual expressions.

In the cleaning process you are again struck by the variation of the weight or thickness of the splint, something you first noticed in the pounding process. Extremely thick splint must be either used in large baskets or subdivided. I recommend that the novice experiment with various weights of splint achieved through the dividing process when weaving a basket. The strength of even the thinnest splint will amaze the maker.

## DIVIDING

When dividing splint, a choice must be made. A practiced user of black ash oftimes subdivides heavier splint *before* cleaning. While the moistened splint is pliable, subdivision increases this pliability and enables a maker to clean the splint with less exertion and pressure. The one hazard is that this thinner splint is more susceptible to be sliced in two. Obviously the splint is not ruined and can be used. It merely shortens the length of weavers and requires more joining in the weaving process. Should these shortened mistakes be of sufficient weight, they can be used to make uprights. DO NOT WASTE THE MATERIAL—IT CAN BE USED. It is easier if you do one step at a time. It is wise to develop a "methodology." First division is done, then all cleaning, and then cutting the weaver strips to the desired width. This will vary depending on the splint.

The first step of division is scoring the splint. Make a quick cut with a sharp knife half way through the splint. I choose to do the cut on an angle but that is not necessary.

*Splint that is damp and flexible cleans easier than splint that is dripping wet. Allow your splint to dry slightly.*
*If pounded splint is of required "heft," a maker will omit division and merely clean and cut to size.*
*If division is necessary, I suggest you adopt my methodology of division, cleaning and cutting.*

Once cut, the splint is folded in half.

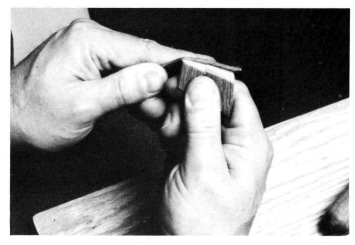

A natural tab (see picture) is formed firmly but cautiously and with equal pressure the splint is pulled slightly apart.

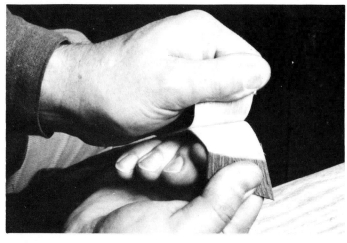

Once started, place the splint between your legs and proceed with the division process. The key to success is supporting the splint with the fingers of both hands and using a rolling, upward thrust of the splint into the area of division. The thumb

actually accomplishes the peeling and when used in conjunction with the index finger, these act as a thickness gauge.

This method at first frustrates most novices, but with practice becomes a rather pleasurable process. An inexplicable joy pervades when you become the master of the material. The weaving weights can be varied by the numbers of divisions attempted. I have on occasion been able to subdivide splint into eight layers. These paper-thin sheets of wood, are remarkably strong and allow the basketmaker endless possibilities; not to mention the satin sheen now revealed with this division.

Some people find this division tedious and tenuous. I have found a dividing box to be a helpful tool especially when preparing a quantity of ash splints in advance. Once the division is started, this box is placed between your knees for support and the splint is thrust up through a widened gap in the board. The box is constructed simply by using two lengths of boards.

**1 of 2**

A shallow channel is cut from the middle of each board and a finish or wax is applied to this channel. The channels are placed face to face and the two boards are nailed together. More sophisticated boxes can be constructed using a spring between the pieces held in place by a bolt and wing nut. When loosened the spring allows the boards to open further so that multiple weights of splint can be divided. On occasion I have also used a vise with its jaws opened to the desired width.

Whatever device you use, the method is the same. In a controlled motion *letting the box do the division*—pull the splint slightly in a downward motion and out away from the opening. The splint is always in contact with the box. The edges of the box can be rounded to encourage the pulling process.

*The channel for the dividing box should be made to accomodate medium splint 3/16" thick. You do not want the splint to be too loose in the box. You might construct adjustable or multiple boxes.*

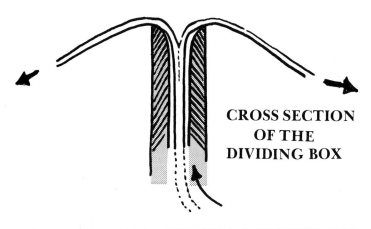

**CROSS SECTION OF THE DIVIDING BOX**

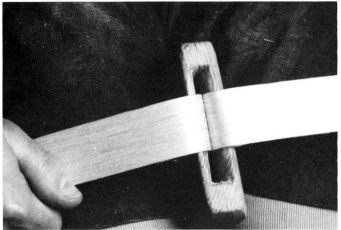

## CORRECTING UNEVENESS

Should you start off not exactly in the middle, the splint will not run off if you pull evenly. If you notice in pulling with the box or peeling by hand that the splint division is uneven, a simple remedy will put you back in the middle. Support the thinner side of the splint and extra tension in pulling is shifted to the thicker side. This uneven pulling will allow you to adjust the thickness back to center. Remember, we all have a stronger and weaker hand and arm, so attention must be paid to this process. PRACTICE IS NECESSARY—as they say "nothing good is easy." Yet the results are worth all the effort.

Should you choose to use manufactured veneered splint or flat reed, these steps are not only unnecessary, they are impossible! The thickness is firmly established by the manufacturer prior to your purchase.

---

*I seldom use splint that is not divided. The satin appearance achieved through division enhances the exterior of a basket.*

## SIZING THE WEAVERS

At this point I usually clean the outside of the splint. I find that by waiting, I minimize mistakes and maximize materials. I cut the materials with scissors or other sizing tools into my desired weaving widths.

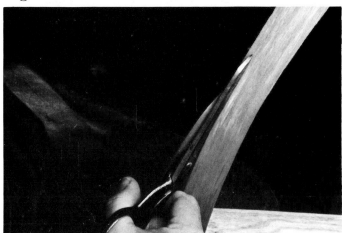

When using scissors, cut a straight clean edge as a reference edge and cut your splint using the edge as a guide. Unevenly cut weavers will produce a poor appearance. Take time to do it right. Naturally, tools with set intervals of blades cut numbers of splint with a single pull.

Should you make or buy other cutting tools, I hope that you begin to enjoy one of the significant benefits of the black ash. Cut fine weavers in your basketmaking. While taking a little longer to weave, you will realize even narrow strands of ash are incredibly strong, resist breaking and greatly enhance the appearance of the basket. Some narrowing of commercial material is possible, but this weakens the materials and complicates its use.

However, black ash weavers store easily and resoak almost instantly. Finally, make sure you prepare enough material. Nothing frustrates me more than starting and then stopping to prepare more material. Sharp scissors are essential! A mashed edge due to poor scissors produces edge frays that should be removed. Careful cutting and cleaning eliminate this additional work.

## SELECTING MATERIAL WEIGHT

When you are ready to weave, attention must be paid to the weight of the material you are using. Unlike commercial materials, you can choose and control the weight of both the uprights and the weavers. I find that weavers approximately 1/4 to 1/3 lighter in weight than the uprights prove to be the best rule of thumb. Too light a weaver and the body of the basket is weak. Too heavy and they weaken or overpower the uprights and complicate proper shaping of the basket. One of the constant complaints that I hear is the lack of material strength in flat reed. A weaver is at the mercy of the material in both thickness and quality. A deft touch and careful handling allows reed to be woven but it makes an inherently weak basket because of the material limitations.

## PREPARATION OF RIM AND HANDLE STOCK

### SPLITTING OUT HICKORY FOR RIMS AND HANDLES

I frequently choose hickory for my own basket production as well as for teaching workshops. This extremely strong wood, when fresh or soaked, flexes well and resists breaking. In 1830 should you be "switched" by the school teacher (rarely done) you were sent out to cut your own switch for punishment. If a child chose hickory there was little chance for it breaking—perhaps an unwise choice!

A hickory tree 7-10" diameter without branches and blemishes is carefully chosen. After felling the tree, cut the hickory at the maximum length needed for your largest anticipated baskets. I oftimes make large farm baskets, so I use 6' to 7' lengths. It is interesting to note that the bark (inner) which rests next to the sapwood (outer section of the tree) can be peeled and cut into strips. These resilient and pliable strips were used to "splint" chair seats.

The diagram shows how I would suggest the initial splitting. If small enough, a mallet and froe will suffice. A combination of splitting, pulling, and controlling the rate of split by pulling and holding the top down with your foot will quickly be developed. The idea is to divide from the narrow

*If using reed slightly dampen the basket before you singe off loose fibers.*
*Store moistened reed in a wet towel.*

*White oak, white ash and other straight-grain hardwoods make great handles and rims. Hickory (Shag Bark) is probably the best. Commercially prepared handles are available along with reed substitutes.*
*Smaller trees often have lower branching or evidence of knots in the bark. A knot interferes with splitting and carving so select your tree very carefully.*
*Shagbark Hickory is found in southern Quebec, Canada and in the Eastern part of the United States. It grows in moist soil and where there is a wide variety of hardwoods.*

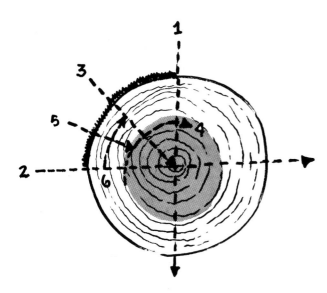

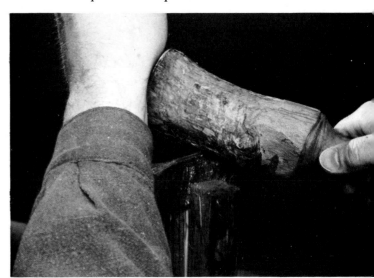

In the picture I chose to use a piece of hickory retaining its bark. The simple removal of the bark is accomplished with a drawknife.

Now using the froe, I strike the back of the blade with my mallet driving the blade into the wood. Once the split is started, the froe is twisted from side to side and slid into the crack until a carefully controlled split is completed.

top toward the bottom and splitting in half the larger pieces either against or with the growth rings. On the diagram, follow the directions of the arrows to split, numbers 1 and 2.

Once a tree is quartered that quarter is again split in half (number 3). The darker heartwood (which I find works as easily as sapwood) is split away from the lighter sapwood (number 4). Then further subdivisions are made always halving pieces until your desired "rough" length and width is achieved (numbers 5 and 6). At this point your stock is ready to be further subdivided into handles and rims unless you chose a small hickory for convenience. In this case you may have split the wood enough.

Because of the strength of hickory's outer bark, it might be wise to remove that for easier splitting. I frequently leave the bark on to prevent surface drying. If I am not going to use it immediately I wrap it in plastic or soak the hickory in a container filled with water.

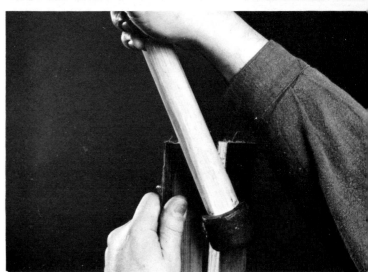

Continue to split the hickory to even sized (squared) lengths. These slightly oversized pieces will allow you to carve all your handles and with further halving, your "rough-sized rim pieces" will emerge.

Determine the maximum outer rim length you require. Our round basket needs about 32" which allows for a fairly sizeable overlap of three inches or more in total.

*Half round reed may be used as a rim substitute.*

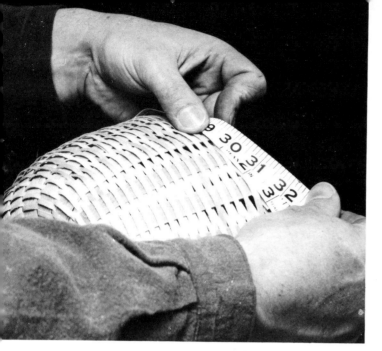

enough.) The following pictures will help you get started. Practice is necessary as with everything.

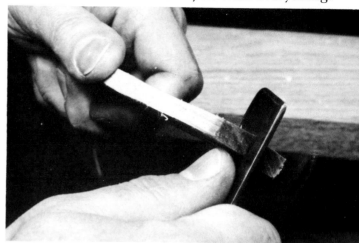

Cut your oversized rim stick to this length and, using a drawknife and shavehorse, continue to size the stick to nearly the dimensions required prior to your final splitting (halving) for rims.

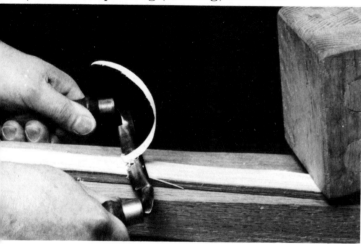

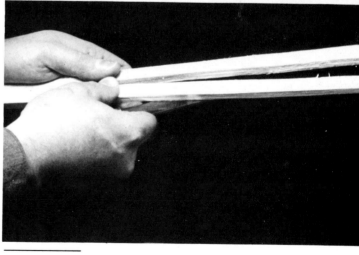

Alternate suggestions are found in the section on Modern Tools and Supplies Needed to Make a New Basket.

After sizing, use a strong flat bladed knife and split the stick into the two pieces needed for the inner and outer rims. Carefully *pull evenly* the stick into two pieces. Should you have difficulty pulling evenly in your lap, clamp the end in a vise. Remember a little pull at a time, NOT ONE SWEEPING MOTION. Pushing against the stick with the "heel" of your palms and wrists while pulling with your fingers greatly aids in control. A froe or strong knife can also be cautiously used if your hands are too weak. (Sawing will probably not work as you may not follow the grain well

*Fresh split wood shrinks less than soaked wood and creates tighter rims when wrapped.*
*A branch from a tree can be carved for a handle, then carefully bent fresh or boiled. A relatively twig-free branch cut in half and boiled may serve for rims.*

## USING WHITE ASH

A good second choice for handles, rims and even splint is the white ash tree.

White ash, *Fraxinum americana*, grows up to 2000' altitudes in the north and 5000' in the south. Its range is from southern Ontario to northern Florida, west to east Texas and north to eastern Minnesota. It is found in moist, well-drained areas populated by other hardwoods. If unavailable in your geographic region, white oak and other straight grain hardwoods can be used for handles and rims. Consult your local library for further information.

*Round reed and other commercially available materials can be carved for handles and rims.*
*Use of carved handles with flat reed baskets may prove interesting. These wooden handles may require forming and drying into shape before using.*
*Tie fresh wood into shape with a cord or covered wire. Rust from uncovered wire is not easily removed.*

## CARVING RIMS AND HANDLES FROM HICKORY

### CARVING THE RIM

Once the rim is "split out", use a piece of leather on your knee and a knife and continue to size and shape the edges as desired. I usually choose the following side profile.

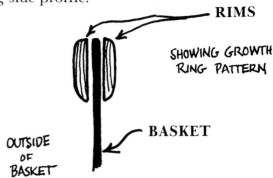

It is not necessary that the flattened side of the rim (side against basket) be cleaned and it is *not* shaped. Our 9" basket as stated before will need an outer rim about 32" long and finished at 1/8" thickness (variable according to basket size). The inner rim will be somewhat shorter. *AS WITH CLEANING THE SPLINT, THE MATERIAL TO BE CARVED IS PULLED THROUGH THE STATIONARY KNIFE AND IS SLID ON A PIECE OF LEATHER.*

*Half round reed in various sizes can be used for rims.*

Sanding can be done; however, quick back and forth scraping motions with a knife also can act as sandpaper.

If you do not intend to use these rim pieces soon, they should be wrapped to prevent drying or placed in a container to soak.

When the rims are finished we begin work on the handle(s).

## CARVING THE HANDLE

The first step is to select a "presplit" piece of hickory and determine the length you need to cut for your handle. The length of the exposed handle is calculated by measuring one half the circumference of the basket. Add to this figure, an insertion amount (part slid inside the basket) for both sides. Our round basket is 5" high so I will use at least 5" for each side. The further inserted the handle the more stable it becomes! The stock is now cut 25" long.

*1/2 circumference (15") + 2 X height (5") = Total Handle Length*

Take care to be sure that the thickness and width of the hickory will allow for the carving process. Many contemporary makers use handles too thin and too high; a critical eye reveals that antique handles were only high enough to allow the arm to be inserted for carrying. Extra height was a waste of wood and effort.

A good proportion of height to width is necessary not only for aesthetics but also for stability. If the handle is too narrow for the basket it will rock from side to side. The handle should be at least as wide as the upright against which it is inserted. Choose a stout upright that doesn't have a folded-over top if possible. The following drawing will give you an example of the shape we are going to carve.

Carving is done on the concave side of the growth ring with the rings parallel to each other. Bending is CAUTIOUSLY DONE by flexing and supporting the wood at critical bending areas. To determine the up and down sides look at the end of the stock, the convex growth rings are to the outside of the handle.

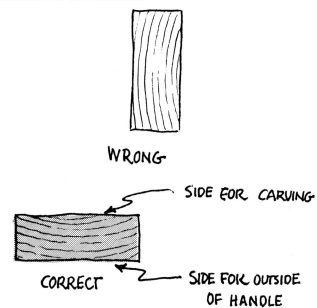

Using your drawknife and shavehorse, place your stock in the jaws of the shavehorse and clean your hickory to size. If you do not have these tools, a spokeshave or jackknife will also suffice.

*The Rough Dimensions of the Stock = 1" wide X 1/2" thick X 25" long*

*CARVE FROM CENTER OUT AND REVERSE.*

*DO NOT ATTEMPT FULL LENGTH CUTS!*

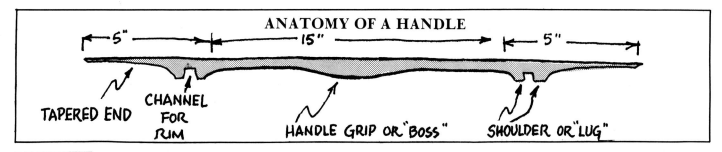

ANATOMY OF A HANDLE

*Handles for rectangular baskets do not follow the formula of 1/2 circumference. They are best* *determined by the function of the basket and the eye of the maker. They vary greatly.*

Now use a pencil and lay out your handle. Locate the middle of the stock (correct side up) and mark in either direction of the center. Add 7½" and again mark, leave a 1½" space either end and mark again. Finally mark a three inch area equally divided from the center for the handle grip area.

*#12 heavy spline, heavy round reed and other commercially available material can also be carved. It is necessary to tie these into position and let*

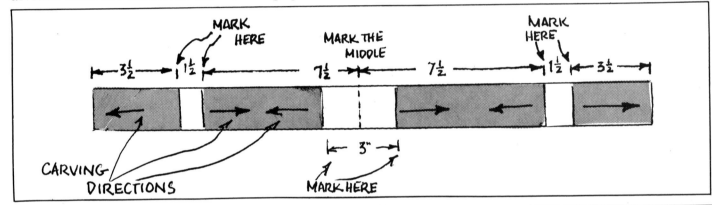

The handle is being carved with a thickness in the center for the hand. This style is often referred to as a "heart handle" in contemporary terms. Because our hands are about three inches wide this will usually suffice and therefore the center of the handle will remain near full thickness. The shoulder areas where the rim channel will be cut also remain near full thickness. See the "ANATOMY OF A HANDLE" diagram.

Insert the handle halfway into the shavehorse and start to remove the waste. *Remove small amounts at a time.* DO NOT ATTEMPT TO REMOVE EXCESS (SHADED AREAS) WITH ONE CUT IN A SINGLE DIRECTION. THE HANDLE WASTE IS SHAVED TO HALFWAY— REVERSED AND THEN REMOVED.

*Mark wood with a soft lead pencil, it is easier to remove.*

*them dry before using them. Should they be used wet, they can easily distort the shape of a flat reed basket. You may find that the use of carved wooden handles with flat reed may prove interesting. Again, tie and let dry.*

Once both ends are completed and the handle resembles our picture and the diagram, you may complete the process with a jackknife. Pulling the handle through the knife, chamfer (round) the square edges. SPEND TIME ON THIS PROCESS! An ugly handle means an ugly basket.

The tapered ends are then slightly pointed and smoothed to ease insertion.

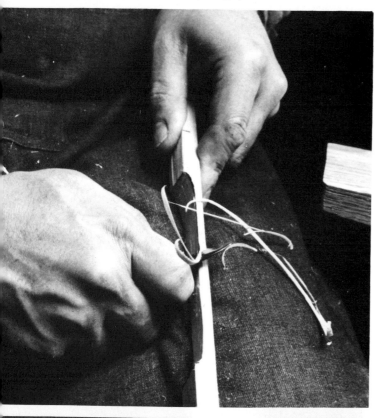

The completed handle is now carefully flexed so as to ease the bending process and prevent breaking. This is done the entire length of the handle or at the place where bends are to happen.

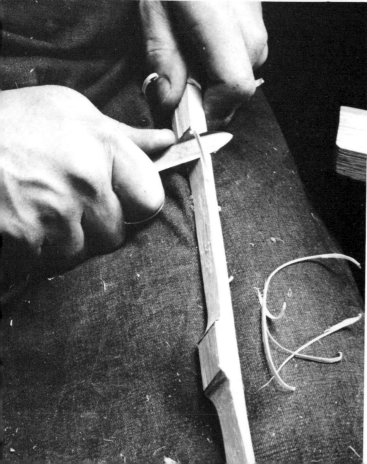

If you are not using green wood (fresh), you may use soaked wood or boil dry wood to promote flexibility. Boiling in a piece of household galvanized rain gutter is easiest. Purchase a length of gutter. It can be hacksawed to the size that accomodates the length of wood you use. Buy two ends and solder them in place to prevent leaking. If you cannot do this yourself, I am sure that a number of "fix-it-shops" etc. can help you with this project. Lay this galvanized gutter across two stove burners and you are ready to boil a handle. A WORD OF CAUTION—fresh wood boiled too long becomes brittle because you have cooked the cells. Five to fifteen minutes is maximum! Dry wood may take up to forty-five minutes or more depending on its thickness. *Constantly check the "flexibility" progress.* It should bend easily without audible cracks. Some waste may crack loose but usually this is only the unevenness you failed to remove and can be carved away without weakening the handle.

*Basket Peddler*
*Woodcut circa 1825*
*Alexander Anderson*
*Print Collection*
*The New York Public Library*
*Astor, Lenox and Tilden Foundations*

30

# Making a Basket

I have chosen the round basket as the first pro-
ct of this section because it is the most frequently
quested style by beginning basketmakers. Once a
aker completes this style he or she can easily
pply the techniques learned to finish a multitude
other baskets. The beauty of basketry is that
ide from different appearances they are all varia-
ons on the three basic styles included in this
apter. The rectangular (page 46) and square-to-
und (page 51) forms incorporate the same finish-
g techniques as the basic completed round
asket. The only variations are in the beginning
ases of these styles and for that reason I have
otographed these steps to provide the maker
ith both pictures and instructions. Once the
eaving is completed the finishing is the same as
e round with the exception of shaping the rim to
rm corners. Let us begin the first basket.

## ROUND BASKET

TARTING TO WEAVE: Using presoaked splint

Depending on the thickness of your splint, you
ormally soak it in warm water for five to ten
inutes, or longer should it be heavier.

Using presoaked splint which you have made
yourself following the instructions in the chapter,
or which you have purchased, the basketmaking
process begins. I have used a round basket which I
frequently make for you to reproduce. The instructions that will follow are for a 12-spoke basket.
This large number of uprights or spokes will
allow you the flexibility of making a fairly large
basket with a strong bottom. Should this prove
unsuccessful for any reason, the same process can
be used with eight or ten uprights.

With the basket on hand, I first determined the
total length of the spokes. Using a tape measure
(something you will discard with a practiced eye),
measure from the top edge of one side of the basket
across the middle of the bottom to the opposite top
edge. This length now requires you to ADD to the
length the amount required to finish the ends
inside the basket. For most baskets, 1½'' on each
end should be adequate.

*LENGTH + (1½'' X 2) = total upright length.*

*Specialty woodworking companies can help with
special needs.*

 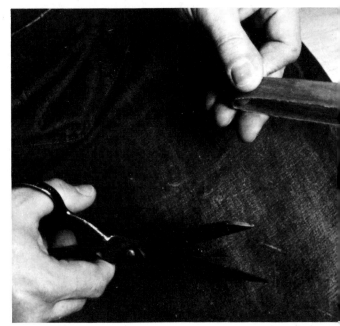

When in doubt make it longer rather than shorter. Our basket totals 22". Now cut 6 strips of at least 2" wide cleaned uprights to the proper length.

Once the 6 strips are cut, they are divided in half lengthwise providing you with 12 fairly substantial uprights or spokes. Uprights narrower limit the basket's strength. *Again wider is better than narrow.*

Approximate the size of the bottom, and usi your thumb as the center reference point, beg shaping the splint in a *very* elongated hour-gla form. A gradual taper is all that is required. rather dramatic taper will only mean the weavi will start closer to the center of the basket. Co tinue to shape the twelve uprights that you cut size.

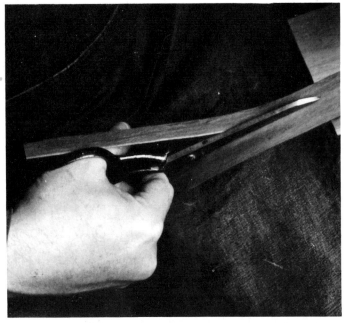 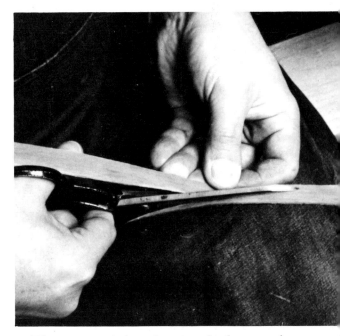

A simple folding in the middle will now produce a reference point for the shaping of the splint.

*Keep a written record of formulas and measurements of your favorite baskets.*

The next step is to lay out the bottom in prepa tion to weave in a "keeper" strip. As the pictu shows, the first 6 uprights are criss-crossed in t middle to produce 12 pie-shaped divisions. N

particular sequence is necessary to make the bottom, however REMEMBER ALWAYS TO PUT THE BEST SIDE OF THE SPLINT FACE DOWN. This will position the best side of the splint to the outside of the basket.

This step requires that you place your top layer of uprights in a sequence and best side down. I have numbered these pieces 1 through 6 to help you complete this step. Choosing a point halfway between one of the "bottom" spaces, lay a top upright in place. Take care that there is no shifting of corresponding ends into an incorrect space. Now continue to subdivide the bottom in a clockwise motion until all 12 uprights are used. At this point you will have 24 small wedge-shape divisions.

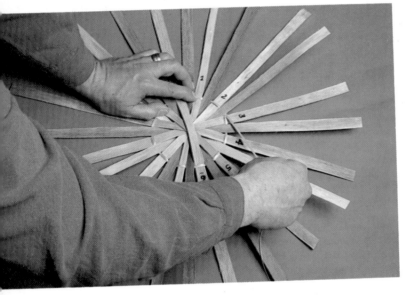

Your final step prior to actually weaving the body of the basket is to weave in a "keeper" strip. This narrow piece of splint is used to lock all members of the basket in place to prevent an unexpected and disruptive shift in beginning the basket. This picture shows the beginning step. Starting halfway over #1 (a topside member) slide the keeper under the next upright (a lower member) and continue this over-under pattern. Special attention must be given to pulling this "keeper" in an even circle and close to the center. Continued adjustment and tightening will be necessary. Once completely around the basket, go over the top of the end that you started on #1 and repeat the process in the same sequence as before. This will produce 2 layers of splint (one on top of the other) and is continued for a distance to prevent unraveling and is then cut.

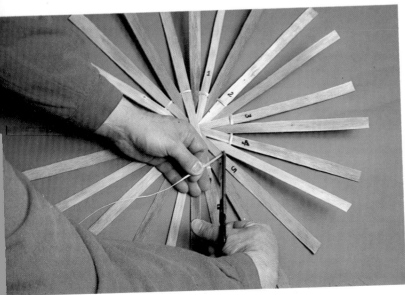

Now you are ready to begin weaving the basket. Because baskets are usually constructed in an upward spiral you will need an uneven number of uprights to accomplish this patterning. (It is possible to construct a basket row by row, starting and stopping as with the "keeper.") Choose an upright that is slightly wider and of good strength and thickness. (This can be preplanned if desired.) In my basket I selected number 6 and using a pair of sharp scissors divide this splint down the middle until you reach the "keeper." *Take care not to cut the keeper in two.* This split will be the starting point and final stopping point of the finished basket.

Choosing from your carefully cut weavers, which are slightly lighter in weight from the uprights, gradually taper the last few inches of the weaver to a point. This taper will allow for a gradual beginning of the upward spiral. This process is ONLY DONE AT THE BEGINNING AND AT THE FINAL ENDING OF THE WOVEN BASKET. Remember to put the best side of the weaver face down so it will be to the outside of the basket.

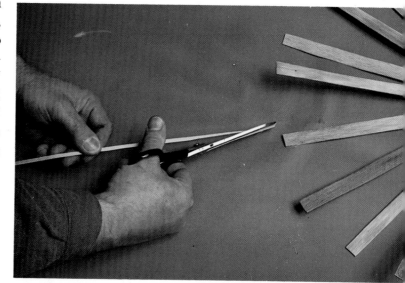

Starting at the split, you will now use these uprights as *two distinct uprights.* Taking note of the need to begin the over-and-under sequence, the "keeper" (first row) happens to go over the splint selected as a beginning point. Therefore, I will slide the point under one of the divided uprights (in this case the right side), tuck the tip under the "keeper" to prevent its "popping up" and begin to weave.

I am now actually weaving and will carefully and tightly weave in my horizontal weavers. As stated, I will now use the split upright as two distinct uprights.

Take care to prevent the bottom from losing its roundness or becoming loose. Concentration is necessary. I use a sharpened stick to enhance the tightening of the basket. Spaces at this point will become greater as the basket dries and shrinks. This splint, because of its grain pattern and how it is processed, shrinks little in length but does shrink in width. Use no extra exertion on pulling this splint except to make it snug. Should the uprights begin to bend upwards you are pulling too tight and you should loosen the material. This area is the bottom and you want the basket to sit *flat.*

When nearing the end of a weaver, a simple step will prevent loose ends and conceal the joint. Stopping at least halfway over the *top* of a rib, cut the weaver off. Select a second weaver noting the correct side. Counting the ending point as one, count backwards to the fourth upright and tuck the end of the new weaver under that rib and on top of the previous weaver. Continue to go over the top of the "bottom" weaver until you float over the cut end and continue to weave as before until reaching the size bottom desired.

*Vary "joining" positions in your basket. It enhances the appearance of your basket.*

Our particular basket will have a 7" round bottom. This size bottom will give a pleasing proportion to the basket and provide sufficient bottom dimension to make the basket stable and useful.

When starting to curve the basket upwards the reason for the use of narrow weavers becomes apparent. The first step is to slightly fold the uprights to encourage their upward direction. Once completed the weaver is then pulled taut. This controlled pulling of the weaver will begin to force the upward movement of the spokes or uprights. Should they not respond, a combined motion of lifting the uprights and pulling the weaver will give them the extra encouragement that is necessary.

*Use of bowls, etc. as moulds or forms can help speed your work.*

38

Persistent, even pulling on the weaver while continuing to weave the basket will begin to form a pleasing upward curve to the basket. Should your tension vary, the weavers in the lower rows will show looseness. Should your tension be too weak, the basket will fail to curve upward at a sufficient rate to produce the projected 9" diameter. (If you finish weaving with the weakened tension you will have a larger basket with a shorter depth.)

At a point that seems logical and comfortable to you, the basket may be placed in your lap. Looking down and into the basket allows you to control shaping.

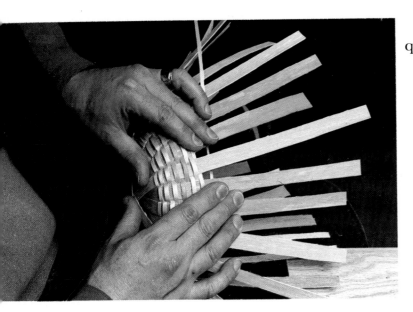

Periodic tightening will prove necessary and a quick view to the outside will show these areas.

Occasionally, the material may slide around a bit from drying. A quick soak will again dampen the splint raising microscopic fibers on the surface that decrease slipping. IT IS UNWISE TO RESOAK FLAT REED TOO OFTEN. IT WILL PRODUCE WEAKNESS OR RAISE FIBERS THAT WILL REQUIRE REMOVAL. Unlike flat reed, periodic soaking of black ash merely helps with the control of your weaving.

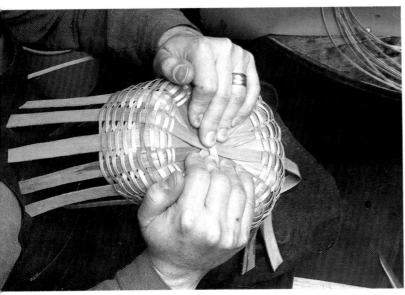

Before weaving the entire basket, attention must be given to flattening the bottom. The bottom is pushed upward with some vigor and encouraged to slightly flex inward. This action will produce a hump inside the basket which helps to distribute the weight of future contents evenly and reduce the pressure on the center of the basket. Pressing the bottom against a flat surface and numerous other invented methods will help to flatten the bottom so it will be level. Should you still have some minimal difficulty with leveling, a final decorative and functional detail (illustrated later in the book) will solve your problem. (See the section on the final detail of lacing, page 63.)

After completing the upward turn, the *need to pull the splint disappears.* Continued pulling will begin to close the basket opening. (Combined planned shaping of uprights and various tensions on weavers give pleasant shape variations for future consideration.) The body of this basket is completed by laying in (weaving) the splint without pressure but *maintaining* its shape. Once the sides are more vertical you will find that joining of new weavers may fall nearly at the same position. Vary these "joins" throughout the basket and not on the divided uprights. *Watch the distances between the uprights* to be sure the basket is even and symmetrical. You will notice now the virtue of narrow weavers when examining the appearance and the minimized "cupping" at the turn.

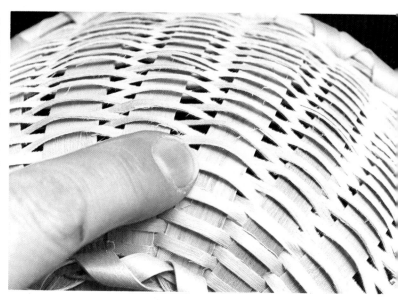

Black ash and other basket materials shrink as they dry. Rather than tightening the basket, as some think, this will produce space in the weaving that must be considered when weaving the height of a basket. I suggest you weave 1/2 to 3/4" higher than you will require and remember that *the rim will be added above* this weaving and must also be considered. When ending the weaving, you will stop weaving slightly beyond the split. The *first upright beyond the split* that allows you to weave behind is the place to stop. Unravel the weaver and taper the weaver back from the end. Start with a point a distance of 3 to 4 uprights and reweave. Our basket is now approximately 5¾" high above the upward curve.

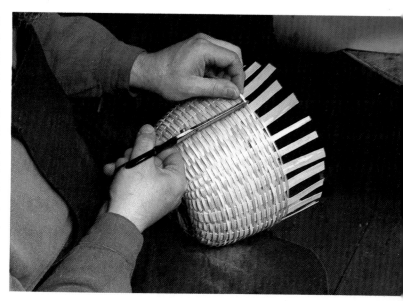

Once the basket has had time to dry (a few days), your next step is tightening the basket. The downward packing of the weavers eliminates unsightly gaps and strengthens the basket integrity.

You may prevent shifting or loosening the body of the basket by *LIGHTLY* misting the splint with water. Excessive moisture will quickly cause the weavers to swell and in extremely fine baskets this unexpected expansion can cause weavers to create unsightly buckles. Redrying may be the *least* of your problems if you aren't cautious.

The final step before finishing the top is adding a rim strip. This wider band acts as a simple device to help keep your basket level and aids in the rim and lashing process. A piece of splint (scrap can be used) which will overlap 2 to 3 inches at the top of the basket is cut to the width of the future rim. Starting at any upright, but *continuing the weaving pattern*, weave in this strip. In order to overlap the end as with the "keeper" (see pictures...page 34) an adjustment in the weaving must happen. A simple floating over or under *2* uprights will be necessary, otherwise the spiral will continue rather than end.

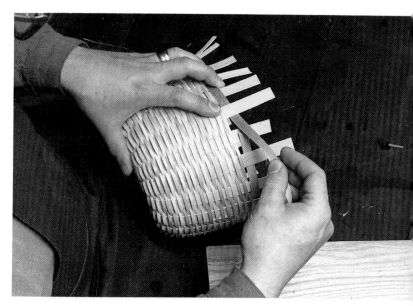

Now immerse just the tops of the uprights into warm water to soften them.

Even the tops of the uprights leave approximately 1½'' to allow for insertion down on the inside of the basket. Slightly point the ends of the uprights that go over the rim strip to allow for an easier job and a pleasing inside appearance.

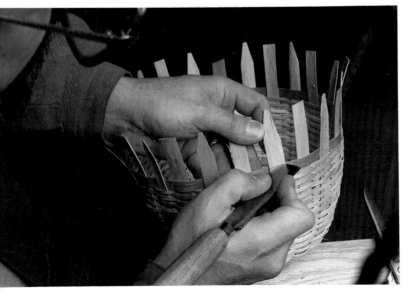

Should the uprights be too thick to bend easily, simply score the top edge and bend over the splint. As in the picture, a tab will appear. Simply pull off the tab and this action will divide the upright making it thinner and easier to insert.

Now insert these pointed tabs over the top of the rim strip and underneath the corresponding inside weavers. This action will lock the rim in place. Indian baskets often have all uprights pointed and the uprights were alternately tucked inside and outside. Yankee basketmakers usually cut off the remaining uprights flush to the top. The basket is now ready for the handle and rims.

For the purpose of continuity we will show how to weave all three styles of baskets before attaching the rims and handles and lashing the basket together. Should you wish to finish this particular basket proceed directly to the chapter on inserting the handle, page 53.

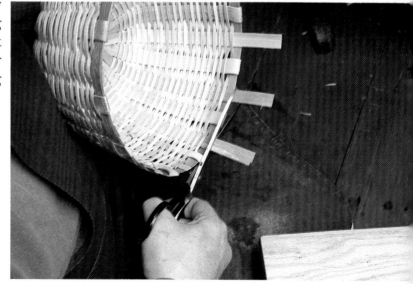

# RECTANGULAR BASKET

Our basket in this section will be 7" wide by 11" long and 5½" high. In a rectangular basket the number of uprights on the handle side must be uneven, otherwise the handle will not be in the middle. I have determined that 13 side uprights appear sufficient and 7 lengthwise uprights will build our basket. Adding our previous formula to the longer uprights for insertion (1½" x 2 ) cut your lengths.

11" bottom + 5½ X 2 (sides) + 1½ X 2 = total end length
7" bottom + 5½ X 2 (sides) + 1½ X 2 = total side length

Once cut to lengths and using the best side face down, place 3 long strips parallel and about 1/4" apart. The need for careful and straight cutting will be apparent. Using a side splint, weave in this upright exactly dividing the end upright in half. *Note that the center "crossed" uprights are equidistant from the middle.*

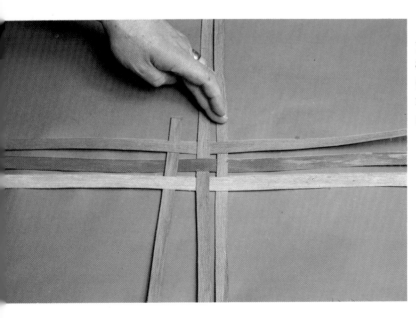

It is this reference point that will help you build your bottom properly and minimize reweaving or adjustments. Now weave in 2 more side uprights. (One to the right and one to the left of the crossed members) *Take care to keep the distances ¼"apart in both directions.*

*Plan your distances between uprights to allow fo sturdy, wide lashing.*

Now weave in 2 more long uprights to the "bottom" and "top" of the base. Again pay careful attention to equal ¼" squares between these members. Continue to weave out from the center until all uprights are used. The bottom or base is now finished except for a "keeper." The unwoven uprights both width and length should be nearly (ideally) even.

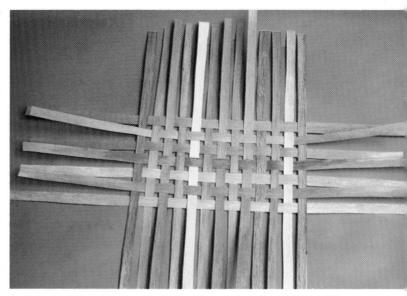

To lock the bottom and prevent shifting during initial weaving, a "keeper" should be added. The narrow keeper will need to be about 4 feet in length and for clarity *one* side has been colored in the picture to show how corners are treated. For weaving in the keeper, you may start anywhere but remember you are "locking" the uprights in place so attention to the over-and under-pattern is necessary. At the corners merely *fold over the keeper.* It is NOT necessary to keep the same side up. Use the color as an aid. As with the round basket, the "keeper" is ended in the same fashion. See pictures, page 34.

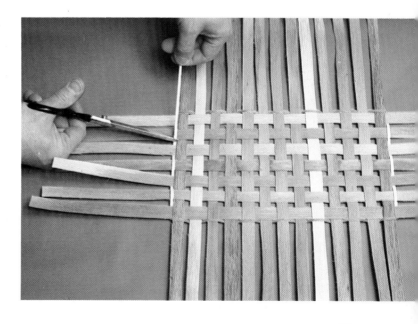

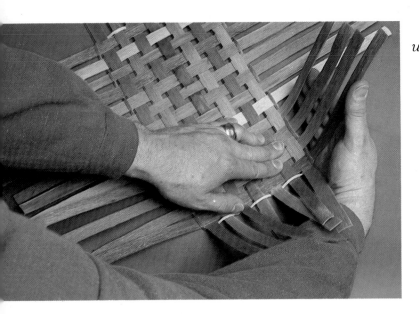

To directly "turn up" the basket, the *WET uprights are folded sharply upright.*

I have chosen to show you a helpful aid in creating an easier turn and neater corner. (You may choose to ignore this step and start weaving directly as we did the round basket.) If you do not want to use this aid *remember do not divide the upright intended for the handle!* See page 38.

Using a wide weaver, approximately the width of the intended rim *(paying attention to the weaving pattern)* start halfway over an upright and weave in this strip. Note that my wide splint has both sides cleaned by division.

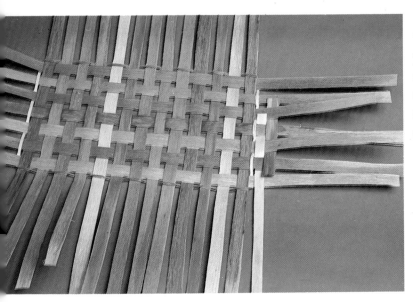

To prevent this strip from popping out a "brake" is alternately woven in above this starting point. This short strip will "lock in" this area for the moment eliminating the need for a clothespin or other cumbersome clamp. Remember periodic spraying with water also helps prevent slipping of ash splint.

Continue to weave this wide splint snug against the keeper. Neatly forming the corners, continue to weave around the basket paying *special attention to forming each corner.*

Once you reach the starting point, remove the brake and for at least 4 splints double over what you have woven and tuck behind an upright. Insert the brake again at this join and cut the weaver off behind an upright as you would a "keeper."

At another position, again weave in a second wide weaver—as always pay attention to the weaving pattern and corners. Finish this second row as the first. Your basket should now be more vertical and with neatly formed corners it will continue to look better as you weave. You are now ready to split an upright to create an uneven number for weaving. Choosing a strong upright, *not where the handle would be placed,* divide this upright to the edge of the wide weaver.

Insert the tapered weaver under or over the split upright (depends on where you start the weaving) and conceal the end into the wide weaver to prevent it popping out. Treating the split again as two, weave the basket in the proper patterned *sequence continuing to use the best side of weaver to the outside.*

Careful attention to tension, spacing and corner will insure a good looking basket when finished. Weaving from the outside and in your lap may help you control this rectangular shape.

End the basket with a tapered weaver and follow the same final steps we previously used to finish the round basket. Review the pictures and instructions on page 45.

# SQUARE TO ROUND BASKET

As the basket in the picture suggests, we are going to start with a square bottom, uneven number of uprights in both directions, and produce a round top. This feat is somewhat accomplished by the mere nature of the material to return to a flattened position. The basket will naturally splay outward if minimal or no tension in weaving is applied. The final rim will insure the round top.

I will be using 14 uprights at least 22" long (This includes all finishing requirements) at least 1/2 to 3/4" wide. OBVIOUSLY ALL DIMENSIONS ARE VARIABLE ACCORDING TO YOUR REQUIREMENTS. Remember, the smallest baskets are the most difficult.

Weave the bottom out from the center leaving ¼" square holes as we did in the rectangular basket. (See pages 46-47) These holes allowed for air circulation and for garden dirt to fall through the bottom. Add the "keeper" as always and the bottom is finished.

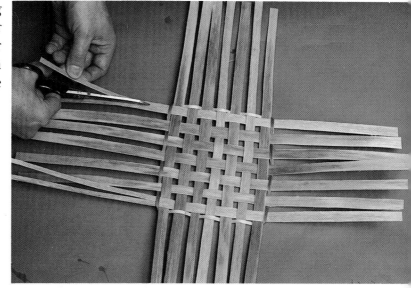

Now split each corner upright into two. You may wish to have wider corner uprights for aesthetics. Because you still have an even number of uprights you must split another spoke. I suggest it is away from the corner and not where you will place the handle.

Inserting the tapered weaver into the keepe[r?]
now begin to *weave using all the divided uprigh[t]
as separate spokes.*

Initial attention to forming the corner is lat[e]
relaxed as the basket climbs. Less and less tensio[n]
is applied allowing the basket to splay out. Th[e]
increasing distances between uprights allows yo[u]
to position the spokes equidistant from each othe[r]
Periodic misting may help in shaping.

Weaving from the outside of the basket, with th[e]
best side of the splint facing you, may pro[ve]
easiest. Periodic adjustment in the weaving wi[ll]
enhance its appearance and roundness.

Finish this and all baskets, with minor e[x]
ceptions, as the two previous examples. Attenti[on]
to drying time, controlled resoaking tops, adjus[t]
ments, all take time but greatly contribute to [a]
finely crafted basket.

Congratulations! You have now completed th[e]
basics that create nearly all traditional Ne[w]
England forms of baskets.

---

*Baskets can be woven from the inside or from t[he]
outside. I frequently use a combination of bot[h]
techniques.*

## INSERTING THE HANDLE

Inserting the "bent" handle means selecting opposite points where the uprights are cut off if possible. Do not choose the divided uprights. Skip a *few* inside weavers and then insert the tab end of the handle under the weavers against the upright and push down. Repeat this process with the corresponding upright. Push the handle down so the shoulder thickness area of the handle is centered with the rim strip. I support the basket against my chest and insert the opposite tab. I find this minimizes distortion. Should the handle pop out, a small misting may help or use a clamp if necessary.

## FITTING THE RIMS

Using one of your "carved rims," carefully flex it and insert it inside the basket. Place it against the shoulder areas. Overlap the ends at least 1½" and slightly away from the handle area.

Now you may cut off the excess overlap and clamp the pieces on top of each other.

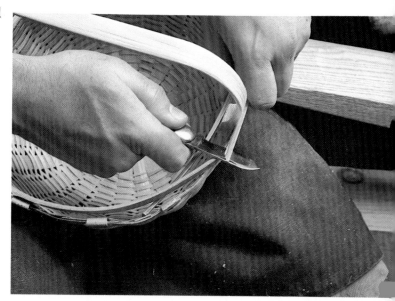

Centering the rim in the shoulder areas of the handle, mark with a pencil on the top and bottom to show you where to remove the waste to accomodate the rim. Mark one side of the rim and handle with a reference mark so you install it in the correct position insuring a proper fit.

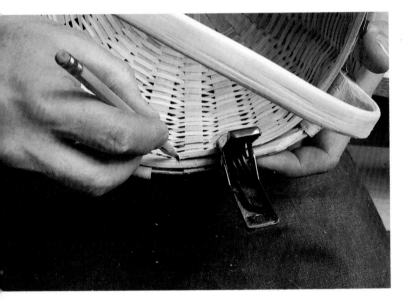

Now you have the channel for the rim marked, again locate with pencil the rim overlap area. Mark top and underneath side to show you where you are to taper the rim ends so they overlap without a bulge.

Using a small saw, cut slightly inside the parallel pencil lines on the handle to insure a tight fit.

Cut slightly over halfway into the thickness and cautiously remove the waste. A small chisel helps or simply use your jackknife. Insert the point (blade) parallel to the top of the handle. At the bottom of the "saw cuts," gently shove in the knife point a *short* distance and twist it. The waste will pop out. *BE CAREFUL THAT YOUR KNIFE DOES NOT FOLD SHUT ON YOUR FINGERS!*

Once the rim channel waste is removed on both sides, reinsert the handle. Return your rim stock to the shavehorse and taper the ends. Remember, they are to lay over each other so the top side of one end is tapered and the underneath side on the opposite end.

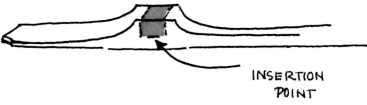

SIDE VIEW OF SHOULDER AREA

INSERTION POINT

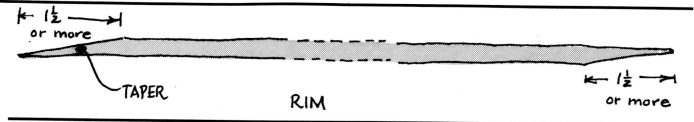

1½ or more

TAPER

RIM

1½ or more

The following diagram shows you how these cut ends will lay over each other.

I have looked at literally hundreds of baskets and have yet to come to any conclusion regarding the direction of the overlap. The taper is to eliminate bulges and to act as a "sliding incline" that allows the rim ends to shift easily over each other as the basket is tightened in the final lashing. Many makers overlap bottom to right and top to the left and carve the rim ends appropriately. I find myself alternating back and forth on this issue. Some makers say this allows for tightening better. I feel if you lash tightly it matters very little, especially if you "cross bind" your rim.

Another observation is that many antique baskets put the inside overlap on one side of the basket and the outside overlap on the opposite

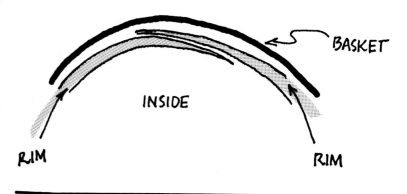

BASKET

INSIDE

RIM

RIM

side. I have been told this helps equalize the basket in the lashing process. Moreover I find that if you allow for a sufficient enough overlap at least *1 ½''*, *preferably more*, on each piece that there is great strength.

If you choose to put the overlaps on the same side of the basket, it matters little. *If you use short overlaps this will not be the case and then joining them in opposite locations will be necessary to help round the basket.* Few antique baskets ever put the overlap at the handle. I suggest overlapping near the handle. The handle acts to distract the eye and camouflage these joins. Experiment and formulate your own opinion! Almost every rule has its exceptions and antique baskets continually provide these exceptions!

The inside rim is inserted using reference marks and then clamped.

Now you lay on the outer rim and again mark it to show the areas needed to be tapered for the overlap. The following two pictures show marking in both possible ways. You are the maker, you be the judge!

Taper the outside rim as you did the inside rim and clamp the rim to the outside of the basket.

If you are using wood that has been soaked for a long time, the wood is "swollen" more than it would be if it were freshly cut. To insure a tight rim, a bit of drying will help. Frequent reshaping during this drying time means that the rim will be round. Minor reshaping after it is dry is possible but *TRYING TO SQUARE CORNERS ON A RECTANGULAR OR SQUARE BASKET AFTER THE RIM HAS DRIED SPELLS DISASTER!*

Now that you have finished this part of your basket let us move on to the lashing process.

## LASHING THE BASKET

When lashing a basket you should plan the style of finishing the rim you intend to use. While not impossible, it is inconvenient to change lashing styles once handles are lashed.

Using a screwdriver, position your inside rim, outside rim and lashing holes so they correspond. Remember you are lashing to the rim strip only. Should you lash into the weavers (except to possibly catch the very end tapered tip) you will make the basket "lop sided."

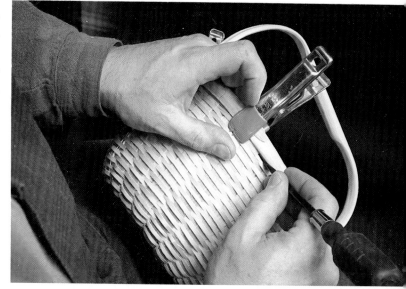

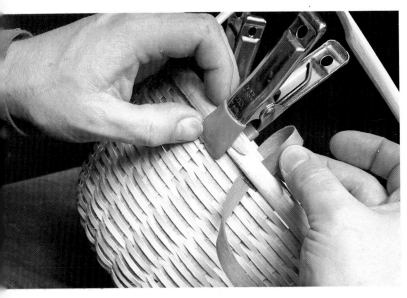

Taking a strong long, (at least three times the circumference of the basket) wide, wet weaver, now called a "lasher" or "lashing-strip," pass the end under the outside rim, under the rim strip and under the inside rim. Loop it over the top of the inside rim and tuck it down between the rims. Pull the long end of the "lasher" tight locking the end inside the rims. **NOTICE I START TO THE RIGHT OF THE OVERLAP TO ALLOW FOR THE RIM TO SLIP AND TIGHTEN.**

Now using the pointed end (done to make insertion easier) overcast the rims to the rim strip

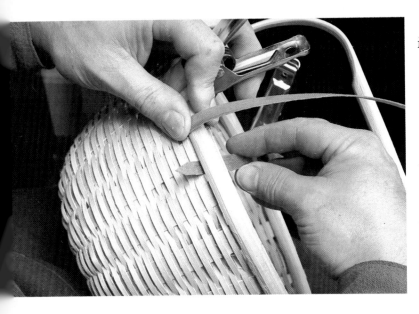

*Circumference equals 3.14 (or pi) times the diameter.*
*Puny lashing strips look weak and are weak.*
*For single bound rims, the lasher should be about three times the circumference of the basket.*
*For cross bound rims, a length six times the circumference will usually be enough.*

Treating each upright individually, continue lashing. Once you reach the divided upright, aesthetics will dictate whether you lash between the "split" or merely go to the right and left. The lashing looks more even by skipping the "center."

At the handle you continue to lash in the same fashion. The rim will hold the handle in position. Some antique baskets merely single bind the handle as shown in this picture.

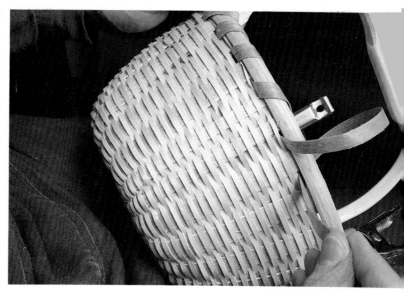

*Collection of Joan Huntington*

Should you want to *cross bind just the handle,* overcast the rim to the outside of the basket once to the right of the handle (left if you are left handed and lashing in the opposite direction). Pull the lashing strip tight and reverse the direction. Cross over the rim to the *left* of the handle forming an X on the exterior of the handle. Pass the "lasher" behind and over the back side of the handle (heading "right") and reinsert the "lashing strip" *through the previously used* right hand opening. Continue to weave as before. Your inside lashing pattern should look like the diagram.

*If you are cross binding you will complete the "X" on the outside of the handle with a wide lasher as you bind the rim the second time going in the opposite direction.*

Continue to lash, tightening as you go, until you complete the first sequence. You now have two options: 1) You may stop at this point or 2) you can reverse the lashing strip and begin to cross bind. Should you choose to end the lasher at this point pass the lashing strip over the top of the rim (final overcast). Come up under the inside rim and between the rim and the basket. Pull tight and insert tip over the basket and down between the basket and the outside rim. Again pull tight and cut off. The process is illustrated in the diagrams.

*Should your lasher show signs of drying, wet it again to prevent breaking.*

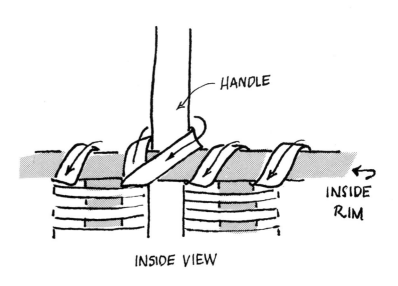

INSIDE VIEW

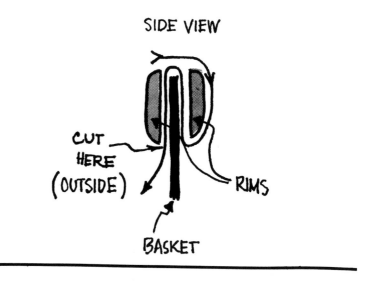

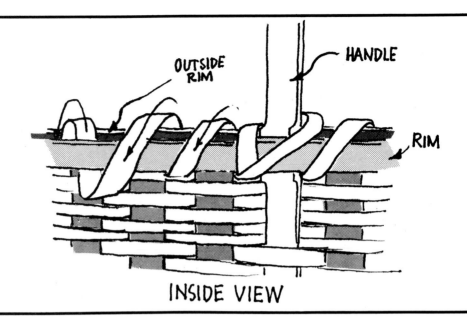

OUTSIDE RIM

HANDLE

RIM

INSIDE VIEW

If you want to cross or "X" bind the rim and were fortunate to find a piece of wide lasher that is six times the circumference, you can complete the lashing without stopping. Once you have completed the first lashing, merely reverse the direction and continue to *weave through the same holes* tightening as you go.

To show starting and stopping, I have chosen a shorter strip and have continued to weave to its end. I have done this rather than stop once around and begin with another lashing strip. Once you reach the handle, you create the "X" on the outside of the handle. The drawing shows the interior view of the lashing at the handle.

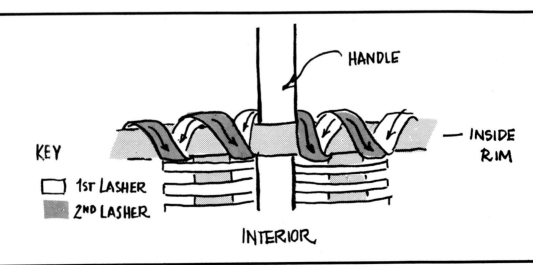

HANDLE

INSIDE RIM

KEY

☐ 1ST LASHER

▨ 2ND LASHER

INTERIOR

*The crossbinding produces an "X" at the top edge of the rims.*

Continue to weave to nearly the end of the lashing strip. Once you reach the last three to four inches, having completed the "X" on the handle, prepare to end this lasher before adding another.

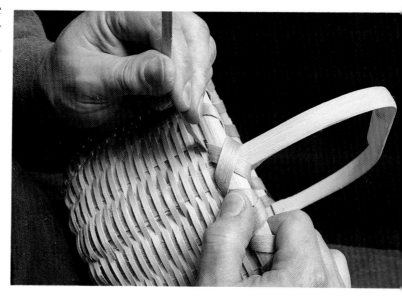

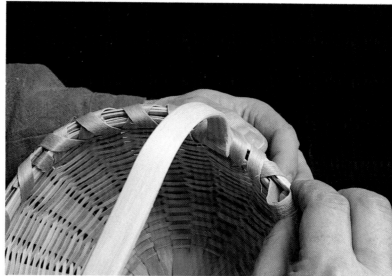

Take the end of the remaining lasher and go over the inside rim, push the end underneath the rim and force up to the inside of the basket. Then pull tight. Reinsert the tip between the outside of the basket and the rim. Push down the end until you see it emerge on the outside below the rim.

Cautiously pull this tip until the excess is taut and disappears. Cut the remainder off.

*Do not join lashing at the handles, stop before or after this area in your basket.*

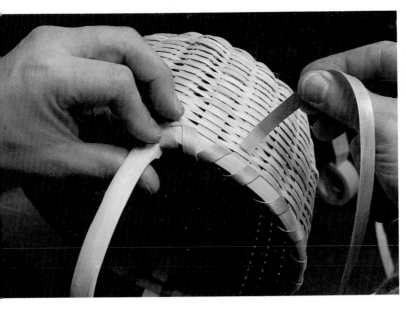

Restarting another piece of wet lasher is done by tucking it deeply under the rim and proceeding further in the proper direction. This tucking process can also be done on the inside of the basket when required.

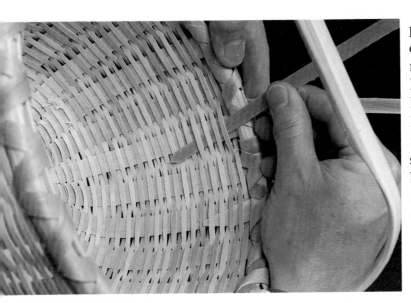

Lashing and ending the lashing tends to be a personal matter. Some makers are obsessed with concealment and go through great care to eliminate ends. To accomplish this they reserve select lashing material that is especially long so that lashing is done with one strip. Others use one lashing strip in one direction and end it, then vary the restarting position and finish the lashing as shown in this picture. The way you finish your basket becomes a part of your style and with many makers as distinctive as signature on the bottom of a basket.

I will show you a way to end lashing commonly found on antique baskets and used both on the inside and outside of the basket. Once you complete the lashing pattern, the end is passed over the top of the rim and then tucked under the weavers and against the nearest upright. Insert the end down beneath four to five weavers, pull the end "out" and pull taut.

Skip one weaver and reinsert the end under the weavers and go over the top of the lasher. Pull the end out at the rim and cut off.

The completed rim is then shaped while still pliable to establish the final appearance of the basket. Check periodically to be sure that the corners (rectangular) are even and to your liking. Once the rim is dry, radical reshaping will prove disastrous!

*The normal drying time for freshly carved rim and handles is approximately twenty-four to fourty-eight hours.*

## LACING

This simple yet effective "foot" was used as a skid that saved the basket from excessive wear and breaking. I have seldom seen it used on antique baskets that were other than round. Placement is obviously up to the maker and if not located on the "keeper" you must adjust this "foot" to accomodate the upward spiral. This adjustment is easily and obviously accomplished once you start.

*Joan Huntington Collection*

Our basket has been constructed so that the "keeper" is the strip that we will use for the foot. Using a wide weaver (cleaned to prevent its abrasion breaking the "keeper") tuck the end under the keeper and underneath a few weavers to hold it securely.

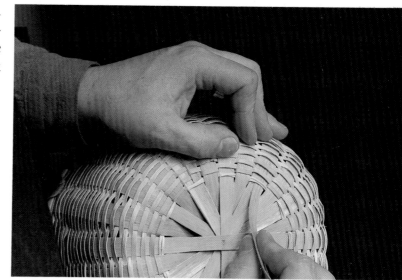

Now simply overcast the "keeper"—being careful not to skip one.

After completing the first pass, go under where you began (a tight fit) and turn the material around and *go back through the same spaces*. This process will produce an "X" bound foot that *stabilizes* the basket, *adds strength,* and looks great!

To end after completing the final crossed "keeper," merely secure the end. Simply passing it under the middle of the basket and underneath an "X" bound "keeper" and slightly up and underneath a few weavers will work well. Should you dislike this appearance do your own thing!

Now you are finished and a signature and (optional) date are all that is required. A waterproof pen shown in the tool and supplies section can be used. I happen to have a personalized branding iron made by one of our museum artisans, but a wood burning tool can also be used. I have found that by deeply burning in my recognizable initials, it prevents some future buyer being deceived as the basket ages.

Congratulations! You are now either a new basketmaker or a converted purist—hopefully both! I trust that the effort has been worthwhile. Remember that basketmakers achieve great leaps forward in their production as they continue to work. Your first basket will become very special to you regardless of how "innocent" it appears.

Successive baskets will build on the knowledge you have gained in making these three basic styles. Regardless of what type of basket you wish to make, the techniques shown in these chapters remain constant. Perhaps now is the time to review the antique basket pictures and unleash your new found talents.

*This antique hanging rack hosts an assortment of antique baskets with beam hooks holding a large rectangular Shaker basket complete with dovetailed runners.*

# Antique Baskets

The following baskets are offered as inspirations to the aspiring basketmaker or collector. These beautiful examples are from the collection of Joan Huntington, except where noted otherwise, and have never appeared in other books. I have not attempted to limit these baskets by the raw materials used or the makers. While New England in origin and all from the mid-to-late 19th century they are a blend of Yankee, Native American and Shaker traditions. I have tried to show forms that recall the styles of the ones made in the how-to section of this book, but on occasion I have included others to show you the extended possibilities.

*Frequently called "feather basket", but that function is questionable.*

*"Feather Basket". Perhaps more appropriate for sewing Indigo decoration on a finely woven basket.*

*Square to round basket. Outside handle insertion bent back to hold. Black ash. (Author's collection)*

*19th century corner cupboard with bitter-sweet interior highlights a collection of antique baskets, candy molds, toys and woodenware. The top holds a finely crafted horse muzzle filled with dried eucalyptus leaves and a charming square to round ash basket.*

*Shaker made. Exquisite. Divided form with great detail.*

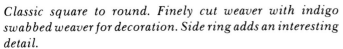

*Classic square to round. Finely cut weaver with indigo swabbed weaver for decoration. Side ring adds an interesting detail.*

*Square to round with higher sides and indigo swabbed split weavers for decoration.*

*Market basket of black ash with indigo decoration. Probably mold woven.*

Low sided round basket with high handle. Swabbed indigo weaver for decoration.

Delicately crafted miniature with colored splint. A low handle inserted to the outside and bent back on itself to hold it in place.

Rectangular with rounded rim. Beautiful handle with colored weavers. Native American made.

Miniature rectangular basket. Black ash. (Author's collection)

Built in 19th century fireplace cupboard holds a selection of ash baskets and folk art accessories.

Indian made. Nailed uprights fastened to wooden bottom. Some colored weavers.

*Footed basket. Interesting handle position.*

*Black ash. Fairly small rectangular basket. Very sturdy construction.*

*Shaker basket—black ash. Form woven. (Author's collection)*

*Possibly New England. Included to show variations on a round basket. Great patina.*

*Ash. Round basket with flared sides. Perhaps mold woven. Extra inserted splints as skids on the bottom.*

*Very dark patina. Sturdy construction. Traces of original paint are visible.*

*Ash. Sturdy round with simple notched handle. Lashing secured to the outside.*

*Possibly Jersey shore. Oak with cane weavers. Extremely strong handle with low sides.*

Aged patina. Square to round. Rim again overlaps to the outside.

Sturdy New Hampshire Swing Handle Basket hangs from a beam with a small pair of baskets on a nearby light stand.

Probably Southern. Unusual rim treatment and shape.

74

*A pair of charming miniature ash baskets quite possibly*
*Shaker in origin.*

*Square to round. Great Age. Simple wide weaver.*

*Deep square to round. Possibly Shaker. Ash.*

*A pair of miniature ash baskets with one showing no evidence of having a handle. Possibly New England. Included to show variations on a round basket. Great patina.*

*Miniature ash square to round. Well made.*

Miniature basket with twig handle. Black ash. (Author's collection)

Black ash basket. Deep and narrow, lined with homespun.

Pair of miniatures with different handle treatment. Note that one has a single inside rim and heavy splint outside. Possibly Shaker.

Shaker made rectangular basket. Oval rims.

Strong sturdy basket with unusual handle position.
Note uprights are tucked to the outside.

Beautiful sturdy basket with fine form and detail.

*Painted a beautiful blue, this machine cut splint basket reflects a growing industrial technology.*

*Shaker. Beautiful dovetailed skid on bottom. Black ash. (Author's collection)*

*Built-in shelves host a grouping of tools, moulds and baskets.*

79

Rectangular basket with lengthwise handle finely woven. Possibly Shaker.

Square to Round. Low sides and high handle.

Rectangular. Note cross lashing on handle is to the insid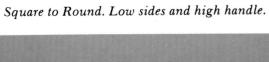

*Slightly narrowed top. Square to round shape in ash.*

*Miniature square to round. Black ash. (Author's collection)*

*Black ash square to round. (Author's collection)*

*A nesting set of round baskets with small carved side handles frequently called "Steeples".*

*No evidence of having a handle. Oak splint.*

*Rectangular ash basket with low sides. Lashing terminates in weavers.*

*East meets West in a simple table top arrangement!*

*Rectangular low basket with oval top. No evidence of handles.*

*Ash splint field baskets amply hold fireplace kindling. Rest-*
*ing on the hearth is an antique mould that once produced*
*basket's shape.*

*Ash. Round basket with simple lashing and crossed to the*
*inside of the handle.*

Black Ash. Fairly small rectangular basket. Very sturdy construction.

Slightly larger miniature. Classic beauty. Possibly Shaker.

Beautiful patina. Note handle detail/inserted on the outside.

*A fine example of painted basketry accessorizes a corner setting. A Staffordshire hen on nest might possibly give a hint of the basket's potential use.*

*Small square to round. Note the knot in the handle. Ash.*

*The top of an 18th century lowboy holds slitting gauges, a Shaker berry basket and a fine miniature backpack basket.*

*...ckpacker Bear made by Chester Freeman with a new ...iniature backpack basket and the three baskets for which ...structions are given in this book, made by the author.*

*Deep square to round with squared off handle sometimes called a "bonnet" handle. Ash splint.*

*Heavy construction with strong rim and handles.*

*A porcupine curlicue basket and miniature ash basket sit atop a Japanese Tansu.*

*Quickly made. Note the handles are nailed rather then held by rim.*

*A Shaker basket with double handles and a miniature market basket highlight an antique 18th century tavern table. African art compliments this peaceful grouping!*

*Beautiful ash square to round. Finely crafted.*

*Stairway study of new baskets on a Shaker peg rack with antique moulds on the steps.*

*Round ash with great patina. Tapered rim slides over the top.*

*Classic round basket—a visual delight. Great patina.*

*Painted ash basket. Some rim separation.*

*Miniature ash with great detail; square to round. Possibly Shaker.*

# Glossary

**Algonkian/Algonquian**-refers to the people who speak Algonquian dialects such as Mohegan, Narragansett, Objibwa, Abnaki, Arapaho, and other tribes.

**boss** a projecting part, perhaps ornamental; often refers to rounded parts; used in handle description

**brake** a small piece alternately woven in (temporary) to retard slipping

**"C" clamp** adjustable clamp that resembles the letter $C$

**chamfer** to bevel-surface formed when cutting away the corner created by two faces (surfaces) of wood; referring to handle and rim detail

**circumference** total outside dimension-perimeter

**cleat** skid; extra additions to the underside or bottom of the basket that prevented direct wear to the basket; easily replaced and frequently employed in antique baskets

**clockwise** in the direction of the hands of a clock; right handed

**coniferous** any tree that bears cones

**cross bind** descriptive; refers to alternating directions in binding; using lashing (lasher) strip alternate directions are crossed over on the top of the rim producing an X at the intersection

**cupping** a term referring to the outward lower flare of weavers at the point of a basket rounding or turning upward

**detail** a small part(s) of the whole; selected area for some special service or finishing

**dividing** to split into parts; our definition will be restricted to equal divisions (halving)

**dividing box** used for splitting strips of ash into progressively thinner strips.

**drawknife** exposed blade with two handles; used for shaving wood. Used by pulling toward the user.

**dressing** cleaning of the splints

**equidistant** equally distant-apart

**felling** cutting down a tree

**fissured** parting; cleaved; split; for our purpose used in reference to the bark pattern

**foot** frequently synonomous to runner, skid and cleat-acts as a "wear barrier"

**gouge** to scoop out a cavity or area

**growth cycle** can be used to refer to one year of growth of a tree or used collectively to refer to lifespan

**gutter** the channel shaped metal used to collect rain off a surface-often galvanized to prevent rusting; *FOR OUR PURPOSES NOT ALUMINUM OR PAINTED.*

**hacksaw** fine toothed saw used for cutting metal

**handle** the means by which a basket is carried; various names were given to styles and some makers added their own personal carving expressions

**heartwood** the center part of the trunk of a tree; wood is darker than the outer sapwood

**horizontal** parallel to the ground or horizon.

**hornbeam** "Ironwood"—very slow growing extremely dense wood in the birch family; hardwood

**increment borer** cutting device turned into a log giving a small tubular cross section of the growth rings

**join** an area of attachment, assembly

**keeper** fine strip woven into the bottom of the basket to keep uprights (members) of the basket in place before weaving

**kicked-up-bottom** the pressed up hump in the bottom of a basket; created in weaving pattern-accentuated by the weaver, it spreads the contents away from the center preventing undue stress; also called demi-john bottom

**lacing** sometimes used synonymously with lashing and binding; refers usually to a final detail

**lance-shaped** like a spear

**lasher** a wide band of splint that is used to overcast (wrap) the rim to hold the basket together

**lug** synonymous with shoulder for our purposes; projects like an ear

**mould** mold, drum, form: wooden shapes over which baskets are woven

**notched handle** our baskets have a groove or

channel cut to receive the rim; a rather loose term—as some "notched" handles are carved with a single shoulder that catches underneath the rim preventing removal.

**overcast** slanted stitch-like lacing

**parallel** equally apart—never meeting

**patina** darkened aging—mellowed surface color from age and use

**peat bog** wet spongy ground

**plaiting** checker board weaving—simple over and under weaving

**puzzle** referring to a mould over which a basket is woven; "breaks" apart to allow for easy removal of basket

**quarter** to divide into one fourth; as in splitting out wood

**reed** available in many forms; flat reed is frequently used as a splint substitute and originates from the center "pithy" section of a climbing palm (rattan)

**reference mark** mark used to line up or reposition in the same fashion—pieces of a basket (*eg.* reference edge, reference point)

**rim** half round or flattened strip(s) with rounded corners that secures handle and strengthens the top; bent while flexible it helps define shape of the basket; certain baskets sometimes use only a single inside rim and wide splint to the outside (*eg.* Shaker)

**rim strip** like keeper but concealed underneath rim. This wide band cut to width of the intended rim is useful for leveling the top. Rim is lashed to this strip.

**sapwood** outermost, lighter more porous wood of a tree and extends to the heartwood

**sawhorse** narrow center beam supported by end legs; rack on which wood is laid to help in sawing

**sawtoothed** having teeth like a saw; serrated edge

**scoring** line or long mark; scratch or incision

**shoulder** ridge or thickness in the handle placed to prevent disengaging (removing) the handle

**sizing** cutting to a specific uniform size(s)

**splay** outward flare; to spread out

**splint** for our purpose wood pounded (black ash) or divided along the growth rings. *NOT THE SAME AS COMMERCIALLY PREPARED SPLINT!*

**split out** dividing wood using wedges, axe, hatchet, froe or other splitting devices—with reference to growth rings

**solder** low melting metal used with a flux to promote joining (cementing) metal parts together

**spiral** upward winding, circling like the thread of a screw; continuous or joined weavers spiral a basket *(Unlike construction which terminates with each individual row using an even number of uprights)*

**spokeshave** small traverse plane-adjustable blade often used for rounding

**subdividing** additional divisions beyond half

**supple** flexible, soft, yielding

**swabbed** wiped on color—as in baskets swabbed with color natural or otherwise

**symmetrical** even; having the same corresponding shape, size, position

**tab** tip or end that "flaps" up

**taper** to narrow, to make gradually thinner toward one end

**taut** tight; to snugly pull

**thickness sander** a sander which allows for specific thickness to be set and attained

**topographical** description of a particular place; graphic survey of land, water, etc.

**transition** a point of departure; to change; passing from one place to another

**triphammer** mechanical device for pounding—more frequently used by blacksmiths; power hammer

**uprights** vertical members of a basket; also called standups, staves, spokes, or ribs

**veneer** thin strips or sheets of wood frequently cut off a log by spin cutting; cut across the growth rings then sized for *commercially prepared "splint"*

**vertical** at right angles to a particular point or surface

**weavers** horizontal strips interwoven with uprights to create the body of the basket

**"works"** reacts, handles

# Useful Information

## NEWSLETTERS AND OTHER PUBLICATIONS RELATED TO BASKETRY

American Craft
American Craft Council
401 Park Ave. South
New York, New York 10016

American Indian Art
7333 E. Monterey Way #5
Scottsdale, Arizona 85251

American Indian Basketry
P.O. Box 66124
Portland, Oregon 97266

Artifacts
American Indian Archaeological Institute
P.O. Box 260
Washington, Connecticut 06793

Basketry Express
R.R. #1
Oakville, Ontario
L6J 4Z2 Canada

Fine Woodworking/Threads
The Taunton Press
Box 355
Newtown, Connecticut 06470

The Basket Mailer Magazine c/o Create A Craft
2961 E. Highland Road
Highland, Michigan

The Basketmaker Quarterly
P.O. Box 005
Belleville, Michigan 48111

The Crafts Report
P.O. Box 1992
700 Orange Street
Wilmington, Delaware 19899

The News Basket
899 Bayside Cutoff
Bayside, California 95524

Newsletter of the Association
of Michigan Basketmakers
495 West Cady
Northville, Michigan 48167

Newsletter of the Iowa Basket Weavers Guild
103 Alta Vista Avenue
Waterloo, Iowa 50703

Newsletter of the Northeast Basketmakers Gui
Post Office Box 144
Bolton, Connecticut 06040

Northwest Basket Weavers Newsletter
3612 Shelby Road
Lynnwood, Washington 98037

For those basketmakers who sometimes feel isolated, the resources above are for your benefit. Each year basket symposiums, conferences, classes and shows occur, these publications will keep you informed.

## NEWSPAPERS FOR THE BASKETMAKER AND BASKET COLLECTOR

Antiques and The Arts Weekly
The Newtown Bee
5 Church Hill Road
Newtown, Connecticut 06470

Maine Antique Digest
P.O. Box 645
Waldoboro, Maine 04572

(Ohio) Antique Review
P.O. Box 538
Worthington, Ohio 43085

As the prices of antique baskets continue to increase, these sources will keep you informed and updated. These papers show many unusual forms and rare baskets which a basketmaker can learn from and a collector can appreciate.

## BRANDING SUPPLIES

Craftmark Products, Inc.
P.O. Box 6308
Marietta, Georgia 30065

Engraving Arts
P.O. Box 787
Laytonville, California 95454

Heat Mark Company
Box 828 Rt 6
Mooresville, North Carolina 28115

Norcraft Custom Brands
P.O. Box 277
9 Short Street
South Easton, Massachusetts 02375

This representative list of resources for branding irons is not intended to be complete but solely a starting point to assist those basketmakers who wish to use such tools.

## MARKETING FOR THE PROFESSIONAL BASKETMAKER

There are many marketing seminars and workshops sponsored by community colleges and other institutions of higher education. Check with the Office of Continuing Education or the Arts Extension Service in the college nearest you. For those who live in New England, I suggest you contact: Arts Extension Service, Division of Continuing Education, University Library, University of Massachusetts, Amherst, Massachusetts, 01003. They sponsor workshops each year. I have found them to be very helpful.

## RESOURCES FOR YOUR PERSONAL LIBRARY

Crawford, Tad and Mellon, Susan. *The Artist-Gallery Partnership: A Practical Guide to Consignment.* New York: American Council on the Arts, 1981.

Halz, Loretta. *How To Sell Your Arts and Crafts.* New York: Scribner's Publishing Co., 1977.

McGuire, Patrick and Moran, Lois. *Pricing and Promotion Guide for Craftspeople.* New York: American Craft Council.

Scott, Michael. *The Crafts Business Encyclopedia.* New York: Harcourt Brace Jovanovich, 1977.

Wettlaufer, George and Nancy. *The Craftsman's Survival Manual.* New Jersey: Prentice-Hall, Inc., 1974.

# Related Books from Schiffer Publishing

**Lightship Baskets of Nantucket** Martha Lawrence. Here the history and makers of the highly prized, distinctive Nantucket Lightship Basket are chronicled, with many color photos that detail construction and show beautiful examples of the craft. Includes what to consider when evaluating antique and contemporary baskets, plus easy-to-follow, step-by-step, illustrated instructions for making your own Nantucket basket.
Size: 8 1/2 " x 11"          120 pp.
over 100 color and b/w photographs
ISBN: 0-88740-256-9          soft cover          $24.95

**Baskets and Basketmakers in Southern Appalachia** John Rice Irwin. American baskets made by people in Tennessee, Kentucky, North Carolina and their surroundings are lovingly shared with the readers by a man who knows and respects their heritage. Indian baskets, especially Cherokee, also are included. Numerous photos detail every step in the basket making process: from the time the tree is cut until the time the basket is completed.
Size: 8 1/2" x 11"          Index          192 pp.
29 color photos, 274 drawings & diagrams, 300 b/w photos
ISBN: 0-916838-61-7          soft cover          $14.95

**The Nature of Basketry** Ed Rossbach. Basket-making is a hand process that has never been mechanized. Hundreds of photos and the text show Asian, American, and European ceremonial baskets, humble work baskets and those made quickly to satisfy a moment's need. Many traditional methods of using plant materials for baskets are described with pictures and discussions of their unique qualities.
Size: 8 1/2" x 11"          192 pp.
51 color photographs          205 b/w photographs
ISBN: 0-88740-059-0          soft cover          $14.95

**International Basketry** Christoph Will. This beautifully illustrated volume presents baskets woven from natural fibers over many years and from diverse American, European and international cultures. Detailed drawings of many weaves will enable craftsmen today to duplicate and experiment with a variety of materials and patterns.
Size: 9" x 12"          192 pp.
405 b/w photographs          31 color photographs
ISBN: 0-88740-037-X          soft cover          $19.95

**Baskets (Revised)** Nancy Schiffer. In this newly revised edition, Nancy Schiffer pays homage to baskets as functional *objets d'art* and includes hundreds of photos of baskets from all over the United States and some from abroad. This pictorial survey of splint, wicker, and coil baskets will familiarize you with baskets used for storage, decorating, carrying, winnowing, gathering and trapping.
Size: 8 1/2" x 11"          Index/Price Guide          176 pp.
190 color plates          143 b/w illustrations
ISBN: 0-7643-0006-7          soft cover          $29.95

**Earth Basketry** Osma Gallinger Tod. Using natural materials, including leaves, roots, reeds, grasses, vines, shoots, willow, bark and splints to create baskets. A wide variety of weaving techniques are clearly illustrated with many examples and instructions for borders, lids, handles and miniatures. Seventy-five pictures and drawings show details, progressive instructions, and finished examples. Novices, naturalists, and expert weavers will enjoy *Earth Basketry*.
Size: 6" x 9"          184 pp.
23 b/w photographs          42 color photographs
ISBN: 0-88740-076-0          soft cover          $9.95

**Let's Weave Color into Baskets** Pat Laughridge. *Let's Weave Color into Baskets* introduces the reader to creative possibilities of adding color to baskets. Chemical dyes are discussed with step-by-step instructions for their use. Many finished examples with color woven into them are presented to stimulate the craftsperson's creativity. Three sets of weaving instructions are included: a field basket, a house basket, and a market basket.
Size: 8 1/2" x 11"          58 pp.
33 color photos          36 drawings          52 b/w photos
ISBN: 0-88740-056-6          soft cover          $12.95

**Indian Baskets** Sarah Peabody Turnbaugh and William A. Turnbaugh. The stunning diversity of North American Indian and Eskimo baskets is thoroughly explored, including basket manufacture techniques, raw materials, forms, and decoration, with information on native lifestyles. More than 175 regional and tribal styles are documented in an easy-to-use and beautifully illustrated format. The book's standardized terminology, identification keys, glossary, maps, and bibliographies add to its broad appeal.
Size: 8 1/2" x 11"          256 pp.
139 color photographs          208 b/w photographs
ISBN: 0-88740-092-2          soft cover          $24.95

**Rib Baskets** Jean Finley. Learn to make a wide variety of baskets in rib-style construction with an authority who teaches novices frequently to love basketmaking. Jean Finley will teach you to make melon baskets, wreathes, doll cradles, and twelve other traditional and modern styles of rib construction. The techniques learned here can be applied to making any style basket. When finished making the baskets, she will suggest other uses and variations that broaden the appeal of new baskets. Decorators and hobbyists will love *Rib Baskets*.
Size: 8 1/2" x 11"          80 pp.
248 color pictures          87 drawings
ISBN: 0-88740-087-6          soft cover          $9.95